The Healthy HomeStyle Cookbook

Ruth W. McGary

 American Diabetes Association.

Printed in the United States of America
10 9 8 7 6 5 4 3 2

American Diabetes Association
1660 Duke Street
Alexandria, VA 22314

Library of Congress Cataloging-in-Publication Data

McGary, Ruth Webber, 1927–
    Healthy Homestyle cookbook / Ruth Webber McGary

    Includes index.
    1. Diabetes–Diet therapy–Recipes. 2. Low-fat diet–Recipes
3. High-fiber diet–Recipes. I. Title.
    RC662.M39   1993   641.5'63–dc20   93-1898
ISBN 0-945448-29-5

TABLE OF CONTENTS

Foreword..iv

Preface..v

Acknowledgments..vi

Introductory Notes 1

Appetizers..5

Soups..17

Salads 31

Breads...47

Meatless Main Dishes...75

Chicken & Turkey...89

Fish & Seafood...107

Beef, Pork, Lamb, & Veal.................................121

Vegetables..129

Desserts...145

Index...176

FOREWORD

The American Diabetes Association *Healthy HomeStyle Cookbook* is dedicated to your good health. We hope that you will enjoy this collection of healthy but fun recipes.

This cookbook is intended to be used within the guidelines of a healthy diet. The recipes are high in nutritional value and fiber yet low in fat, cholesterol, and sugar and relatively low in sodium. Even though American Diabetes Association–approved exchanges are given for each recipe to assist individuals with special dietary needs, the delicious foods in these recipes are meant for everyone. We hope that you have fun mixing and matching recipes to come up with meals you will feel good about serving.

The American Diabetes Association *Healthy HomeStyle Cookbook* was originally developed under the auspices of the Central Maine Power Company and donated to the Kennebec Valley Chapter of the American Diabetes Association Maine Affiliate, who felt that these recipes were too good not to share with the rest of us!

American Diabetes Association

The recipes in this book were created for people interested in a healthy diet of foods high in fiber and taste appeal, yet low in fat, cholesterol, and sugar. Most of the recipes are relatively low in sodium. The ingredients are available in most supermarkets and health food stores, and some can be grown in your home garden.

Most of the foods will be familiar to you. However, a spirit of adventure may put you in the mood to try some new ways to prepare old favorites, perhaps some that you may have been avoiding lately, such as dips or cheesecakes. It is interesting to note that the recipes calling for eggs were tested using several low-cholesterol egg substitutes with satisfactory results in all cases.

I hope you enjoy using this unique guide to a healthy diet as much as I enjoyed preparing it for you. I am delighted to share with you some of the recipes that help me control my type II diabetes.

My sincere thanks to family, friends, and colleagues who ate their way through the recipes in this collection.

Ruth W. McGary
Home Economist
Winthrop, Maine

ACKNOWLEDGMENTS

The American Diabetes Association gratefully acknowledges the following contributors to *The Healthy HomeStyle Cookbook*.

The following people were taste testers:

Carroll McGary   Althea & Richard Hoisington
Laura Bailey   Lil & Paul Rourke
Carol Varnam   Rachel Hall
Priscilla Stevenson   Thomas, Kelly, & Caleb McGary
Jeanne Nason   Isabelle & John Weber
Ramona Carson   Donna & Emeth McGary
Brenda Eddy   Eric Lindquist

Careful nutritional analysis and exchange calculations were performed by Delia Hyland, MA, RD, LD. We are grateful to Susan Thom, RD, LD, CDE, for additional taste testing and nutritional analysis.

Sue Thomas, President of the Kennebec Valley Chapter of the ADA Maine Affiliate; Lynn K. Goldfarb, Vice President of Marketing, Central Maine Power Company; and Elizabeth Swenson and Rick Johnston of the ADA Maine Affiliate were responsible for bringing this cookbook to the attention of the American Diabetes Association Publications Division.

The manuscript was reviewed by Karmeen Kulkarni, RD, MS, CDE, and Larry Deeb, MD. This cookbook was produced by Christine B. Welch, Managing Editor; Sherrye Landrum, Associate Editor; and Susan H. Lau, Publisher. Cover photograph is by Fil Hunter. Food was prepared by Susan Foresman. Book design is by Tom Suzuki, Inc., and Insight Graphics, Inc.

Whole eggs in cooked foods can usually be replaced with egg whites or a non-fat, low-cholesterol egg substitute found in grocery stores or with this home-made version.

Low-Cholesterol Egg Substitute:
1   Tbsp. nonfat dry milk granules
2   large egg whites
2   drops yellow food color

Combine and beat until smooth. Equivalent to 1 large egg.

CREAM CHEESE can often be replaced with YOGURT CHEESE, made by draining 4 cups of low-fat yogurt in a colander lined with several layers of cheesecloth (found in the housewares section of the supermarket). Set over a bowl, cover, and place in the refrigerator overnight. There will be about 1 1/2 cups of yogurt cheese on the top. The whey in the bowl can be used in soups or baked goods such as whole-wheat bread.

SOUR CREAM can often be replaced (in dips and sauces) by low-fat yogurt. To keep yogurt from separating in foods that will be cooked, add 1 teaspoon of cornstarch per cup of yogurt.

The fresh fruits and vegetables called for in this book may seem quite costly, but actually are less expensive than many ingredients high in cholesterol, fat, sodium, and sugar.

BUTTER AND REGULAR MARGARINE have an equal number of calories, but REDUCED-CALORIE MARGARINE may have up to 50% less fat and calories. Choose a diet or lite brand for vegetables and most baking. For toast and hot bread, choose a standard margarine with a higher percentage of unsaturated fat than saturated fat.

Poly- and monounsaturated fats such as CORN, SAFFLOWER, SUNFLOWER, and CANOLA oils are recommended as all-purpose oils. Use others in small amounts for special purposes.

Coat baking and frying pans with a NONSTICK VEGETABLE COOKING SPRAY. Use a light coat on cookie sheets, jelly roll pans, cake pans, muffin cups, bread pans, electric skillet, casseroles, omelet pans, custard cups, and containers for leftovers.

Most meats lose about 25 percent in weight in the cooking process. For example, 4 ounces of raw lean ground beef will be a 3-ounce portion of cooked meat.

Saute in the MICROWAVE OVEN without fat. Usually there is enough moisture in or on the food to provide juices for cooking. Chop food as usual, spread in a covered casserole, and consult the recipe manual for your oven for time. Use the automatic cooking feature if you have one.

Team up the MICROWAVE OVEN with conventional methods and with the WOODSTOVE. Do the slow-cooked recipes when heat is needed in the house. Reheat individual portions by microwave.

Canned milk or nonfat dry milk can usually be used in place of fresh milk. In recipes calling for evaporated milk, substitute evaporated skim milk.

Save all the water that vegetables are cooked in by collecting it in covered containers and storing in the freezer until needed for soups and sauces. Thaw in the refrigerator overnight or on the warming shelf over the woodstove.

Save the crumbs left from making party-mix cereal mixtures that are seasoned with margarine, spices, herbs, and Worcestershire. Collect crumbs in a freezer container and use for casserole toppings. Omit butter and seasonings called for in the topping.

LITE soy sauce refers to the reduced-sodium sauce, not to be confused with LIGHT, which refers to color.

Stock up on BAKING SODA when it is on sale. Use it as a cleaning powder for counter tops; refrigerator, inside and out; coffee or tea stains on plastic; burned-on food in a cooking kettle (1/4 cup baking soda and 1 cup of water; simmer 5 to 10 minutes); odor-eater in sneakers; and emergency toothpaste.

When BANANAS are on special, freeze perfectly ripened ones for use in baked goods later on. Separate them and place loose bananas in airtight bags. To use, thaw (preferably in refrigerator), and cut off one end and squeeze out like toothpaste. You have ready-to-use mashed banana.

Use KITCHEN SHEARS to snip parsley and chives, to slice small green onions and stems, to cut spinach and lettuce into strips, and to trim pastry.

Freeze your surplus TOMATOES (whole or cut up) on large baking pans. When hard, transfer to freezer-safe plastic bags. To use, weigh out the amount called for in recipes.

Many recipes call for CHICKEN STOCK. Homemade tastes best and is least expensive. You can chill it and skim fat from the top to keep it low in fat. You can also control the sodium content better when you're cooking. But if you're in a hurry, here are some alternatives. Stores offer low-sodium canned chicken broth. Before opening, set the can in the refrigerator for an hour, then after opening, lift the fat off the top. Low-sodium chicken bouillon granules or cubes are also available. After preparing, cool and skim the fat before using.

Experts on good health agree that you should get, on average, less than 30 percent of your total daily CALORIES FROM FAT. A simple way to meet this goal would be to select only recipes that contain 30 percent or less of their calories from fat. Look for the percentage of calories from fat in parentheses at the bottom of each recipe. But oils, margarine, and dressings (100 percent of their calories are from fat) or some recipes may provide more than 30 percent of calories from fat. What do you do? For healthy eating, limit yourself to 1 tablespoon of a food that gets 100 percent of its calories from fat. And if the dish you want to prepare has more than 30 percent of calories from fat, complete that meal with low-fat foods. The number you are most concerned with is the amount of fat that you eat in one whole day, not in just one dish.

Recipes in the *Healthy Homestyle Cookbook* that need to be balanced by including lower-fat foods in that meal or at other meals that day are marked with this symbol:

⚖ Balance with lower-fat dishes on days you use this recipe.

Don't skip over these recipes! Just use them as one part of a meal along with low-fat foods, such as fresh fruit salads, crusty sourdough rolls without margarine, and steamed fresh vegetables with herbs for seasoning.

Recipes for occasional use because of SODIUM content (those with more than 400 milligrams of sodium per serving) are marked with an asterisk *.

Recipes for occasional use due to SUGAR content are also marked with an asterisk*. These recipes yield foods that contain between 1 teaspoon and 1 tablespoon of sugar per serving. Limit yourself to one servng of these foods per day. Many sweeteners are available for use in your cooking, such as table sugar, honey, molasses, corn syrup, or sugar alcohols (mannitol and sorbitol), but keep track of the amount of sweetener per serving. Recipes with less than 1 teaspoon of a caloric sweetener PER SERVING can be used regularly. Remember not to use aspartame (Equal or NutraSweet) as a sugar substitute in foods that will be baked.

SWEET AND SOUR MEATBALLS*

7 Servings/Serving size: 3 meatballs

Save the extra sauce and refrigerate it in a covered bowl. Lift off any fat that congeals on the top and use the sauce for another batch of meatballs. This sauce may be frozen.

INGREDIENTS

1	lb. lean ground beef or turkey	
1	small onion, chopped	
1/4	cup egg substitute or 1 egg	
1/2	tsp. salt (optional)	
1/4	tsp. pepper	
2	Tbsp. water	

Sauce:
1 small onion, chopped
1   cup catsup
1 1/2 Tbsp. brown sugar or equivalent noncaloric artificial sweetener
1 1/2 Tbsp. lemon juice
1 Tbsp. lite soy sauce

METHOD

1. Combine all meatball ingredients; mix well. Shape into 20 (1-inch) meatballs. Place in 9-inch baking dish. Microwave 8–9 minutes on MEDIUM-HIGH (70% power); drain and rearrange meatballs.
2. Pour sauce over meatballs and continue cooking 3–5 minutes on MEDIUM-HIGH (70% power), or until hot.

To make sauce:
1. Place onions in 1-qt. measuring cup or bowl.
2. Microwave 2–3 minutes on HIGH or until onion is partly cooked. Stir in remaining ingredients.

⚖ Balance with lower-fat dishes on days you use this recipe. *Not recommended for low-sodium diets.

Including the sauce:
Starch/Bread Exchange 1
Medium-Fat Meat Exchange 1
Calories 166
Carbohydrate ....14 grams
Protein ....11 grams
Fat.................................7 grams (38%)

Saturated fat ....2.5 grams
Cholesterol........................30 milligrams
  with egg ....60 milligrams
Fiber.......................................0.61 grams
Sodium............................574 milligrams
Without added salt..........410 milligrams

6 Servings/Serving size: 1/4 cup

Yes, low-fat clam dip! The secret ingredient is yogurt cheese, but if it isn't mentioned, even folks who don't like yogurt will go back for more. Yogurt cheese is drained yogurt, thicker and more tangy than regular yogurt. Start one day in advance. Set a fine mesh strainer over a bowl. (Line strainer with cheese cloth if the mesh is large.) Spoon in three cups low-fat plain yogurt. Cover and refrigerate overnight. The solid in the strainer is yogurt cheese. The whey in the bowl may be used in place of buttermilk in bread.

INGREDIENTS

1	can (6 1/2 oz.) chopped clams
1	cup yogurt cheese (see above)
1/2	tsp. Worcestershire sauce
1/8	tsp. freshly ground pepper

METHOD

1. Drain juice from clams and reserve.
2. Beat cheese until smooth.
3. Add clams, Worcestershire, and pepper and clam juice as needed for dip consistency. Serve immediately or chill.

Lean Meat Exchange 1	Saturated fat ....0 grams
Calories 38	Cholesterol ....14 milligrams
Carbohydrate ....2 grams	Fiber... 0 grams
Protein ....5 grams	Sodium........................... 215 milligrams
Fat ....1 gram (23%)	

SPINACH-ONION DIP

9 Servings/Serving size: 1/4 cup

This is a creamy, yet low-fat base for many dips. Instead of spinach you can add other vegetables, herbs, and seasonings. Serve with fresh, crisp vegetables, such as carrots, celery, sweet peppers, asparagus, broccoli, or cauliflower. Prepare at least 4 hours in advance so the flavors can develop. This dip is also good to fill an omelet or as a topping for baked potatoes. For a creamy salad dressing, thin dip with a little flavored vinegar such as tarragon, add some calorie-reduced salad dressing, and serve over individual tossed salads.

INGREDIENTS

10	oz. fresh spinach or 1 pkg. frozen, chopped and thawed
1	cup 1% low-fat cottage cheese
1	Tbsp. lemon juice
1/2	cup low-fat plain yogurt
1/2	cup chopped fresh parsley
1/4	cup chopped scallions, including 2 inches green tops, or 1/4 cup chives
1/4	tsp. salt (optional) Freshly ground pepper

METHOD

1. Trim stems and coarse leaves from spinach. Rinse spinach and cook covered over medium heat for 3 minutes or until wilted. (If using frozen, no need to cook.)
2. Thoroughly drain spinach, squeezing out excess moisture; coarsely chop and set aside.
3. In blender or food processor, process cottage cheese with lemon juice until blended. Add spinach, yogurt, parsley, scallion, salt, and pepper to taste; process just until mixed.
4. Cover and refrigerate for at least 4 hours or overnight to blend flavors.

Lean Meat Exchange	1	Saturated fat	0.3 grams
Calories	45	Cholesterol	2 milligrams
Carbohydrate	4 grams	Fiber	1.5 grams
Protein	5 grams	Sodium	172 milligrams
Fat	1 gram (20%)	Without added salt	108 milligrams

BROCCOLI AND MUSHROOM DIP

12 Servings/Serving size: 1/4 cup

A low-calorie, high-fiber dip for veggies. Also good as a topping for baked potatoes.

INGREDIENTS

2   cups broccoli, chopped
1   clove garlic, minced
1   small onion, chopped
1/4 lb. fresh mushrooms,
     chopped
2   tsp. corn oil
1   cup 1% low-fat cottage cheese
     Freshly ground pepper

METHOD

1. Cook broccoli until tender-crisp (2 minutes in the microwave, if you have one). Drain.
2. In a small skillet cook garlic, onions, and mushrooms in oil for about 5 minutes, until onion is tender (or 2–3 minutes in the microwave oven).
3. In food processor or blender process cottage cheese until smooth. Add pepper and vegetables. Process until mixed.
4. Cover and refrigerate. Will keep for 2 days.

Vegetable Exchange 1	Saturated fat ....0.22 milligrams
Calories 29	Cholesterol.........................8 milligrams
Carbohydrate ....2 grams	Fiber...0 grams
Protein ....3 grams	Sodium.............................66 milligrams
Fat.....................................1 gram (31%)	

YOGURT CHEESE "BOURSIN"

6 Servings/Serving size: 1/4 cup

If you like the flavor of Boursin cheese but have been avoiding it because of the calories, try this version. Use it as a spread on crackers, a dip for veggies, or a topping for baked potatoes. Yogurt cheese can be used plain as a replacement for cream cheese on bagels and English muffins and in uncooked concoctions.

INGREDIENTS

1 1/2 cups yogurt cheese (see
    page 1)
1   clove garlic squeezed through
    garlic press
1/2   tsp. oregano
1/4   tsp. thyme
1/4   tsp. basil
1/4   tsp. marjoram
1/4   tsp. dill weed

METHOD

1. Make yogurt cheese by spooning 4 cups low-fat yogurt into a cheese cloth–lined strainer set over a bowl. Cover and refrigerate overnight.
2. Turn the solids into a bowl, add the seasonings, and beat until smooth.

Lean Meat Exchange 1/2	Saturated fat ....0 grams
Calories 33	Cholesterol.........................10 milligrams
Carbohydrate ....2 grams	Fiber...0 grams
Protein ....4 grams	Sodium.............................20 milligrams
Fat.....................................1 gram (27%)	

ZUCCHINI PIZZAS

For the adventurous vegetable lovers out there.

INGREDIENTS

2   fresh zucchini, about 2 inches in diameter, cut into 1/4-inch slices

On each slice place in order:

1   Tbsp. pizza sauce
1   tsp. black olives, chopped
1   tsp. green onion, minced
2   Tbsp. fat-free mozzarella, grated

METHOD

1. Place on a baking sheet and broil until cheese is melted and bubbly, about 3–5 minutes. Zucchini should be crisp.

Lean Meat Exchange............................1	Saturated fat....................................trace
Calories 53	Cholesterol ....1 milligram
Carbohydrate ....5 grams	Fiber ....1 gram
Protein ....6 grams	Sodium............................373 milligrams
Fat ....1 gram (17%)	

FRESH VEGETABLE DIPPERS

8 Servings/Serving size: 1/2 cup veggies with 1/2 Tbsp. sauce

INGREDIENTS

8	oz. fresh mushrooms
1	lb. fresh broccoli
1	lb. fresh cauliflower
3	Tbsp. reduced-calorie margarine
1/8	tsp. garlic powder
1/4	tsp. seasoned salt (optional)
1	Tbsp. lemon juice

METHOD

1. Clean and trim vegetables; cut into bite-size pieces. Arrange vegetables on a platter, leaving space in center for sauce.
2. Combine sauce ingredients in 6-ounce custard cup or dish; place in center of platter. Cover platter with plastic wrap.
3. Microwave 8–9 minutes on HIGH until vegetables are tender. Remove plastic wrap. Stir sauce.
4. Dip veggies into sauce. Dieters may have to dip very lightly. Provide napkins for drippings.

Vegetable Exchange 1	Saturated fat ....trace
Calories 34	Cholesterol..........................0 milligrams
Carbohydrate ....3 grams	Fiber ....1 gram
Protein.....................................1 gram	Sodium...........................122 milligrams
Fat...................................2 grams (53%)	Without added salt............42 milligrams

SPINACH AND CHEESE SQUARES

18 Servings/Serving size: 2 squares

Nutritious nibblers that can be made ahead and refrigerated or frozen, then reheated at party time.

INGREDIENTS

1/2	cup egg substitute or 2 eggs
6	Tbsp. whole-wheat flour
1	pkg. (10 oz.) frozen chopped spinach, thawed and well drained
2	cups 1% low-fat cottage cheese
2	cups low-fat cheddar cheese, grated
1/2	tsp. freshly ground pepper
1/8	tsp. cayenne or to taste Pinch nutmeg (optional)
3	Tbsp. wheat germ

METHOD

1. In a large bowl beat the egg substitute with the flour until the mixture is smooth
2. Add the spinach, cheeses, cayenne and nutmeg, and mix the ingredients well. Pour mixture into a vegetable cooking spray-coated 13 x 9 x 2-inch baking pan.
3. Sprinkle the top with wheat germ and bake at 350° for about 45 minutes.
4. Let stand for about 10 minutes and then cut into 1 1/2-inch squares for serving.

Lean Meat Exchange	1	Saturated fat	1 gram
Calories	66	Cholesterol	14 milligrams
Carbohydrate	4 grams	with egg	38 milligrams
Protein	8 grams	Fiber	1 gram
Fat	2 grams (27%)	Sodium	303 milligrams

HEARTY ZUCCHINI HORS D'OEUVRES

32–48 Servings/Serving size: 1 slice

An interesting way to serve fresh or frozen zucchini as an appetizer or to accompany soup or salad. Makes about 48 rye bread hors d'oeuvres or 32 French bread toasts.

INGREDIENTS

2	cups shredded zucchini, fresh or frozen, thawed
1	tsp. salt (optional)
1/2	cup reduced-calorie mayonnaise or salad dressing
1/2	cup low-fat plain yogurt
1/4	cup grated Parmesan cheese
4	scallions, thinly sliced
1	tsp. Worcestershire sauce
1	clove garlic, minced
4	drops hot pepper sauce
48	slices of party rye bread or 32 French bread slices

METHOD

1. In a medium mixing bowl, stir together zucchini and salt. Let stand one hour. Drain; rinse; drain well, pressing out excess liquid.
2. Stir together zucchini, mayonnaise or salad dressing, yogurt, cheese, green onions, Worcestershire, garlic, and hot pepper sauce.
3. Spread 1 1/2 teaspoons of the zucchini mixture on each rye bread slice or 2 1/2 teaspoons of the zucchini mixture on each French bread slice.
4. Place on a baking sheet. Bake in a 375° oven for 12 minutes. Serve immediately.

Starch/Bread Exchange	1	Saturated fat	1 gram
Fat Exchange	1/2	Cholesterol	2 milligrams
Calories	95	Fiber	1 gram
Carbohydrate	14 grams	Sodium	260 milligrams
Protein	3 grams	Without added salt	188 milligrams
Fat	3 grams (28%)		

MARINATED CELERY, GREEK STYLE

8 Servings/Serving size: 1/2 cup

Spear this cool vegetable appetizer on toothpicks to serve a crowd or as a side dish for a buffet meal.

INGREDIENTS

4	cups celery, cut diagonally into 1 1/2-inch pieces
1/4	cup olive oil
	Juice of 1 lemon
2	Tbsp. fresh fennel leaves, chopped, or 1 tsp. dry fennel seed
1–2	sprigs fresh thyme, chopped or pinch of dry thyme
2	sprigs fresh parsley, chopped
1	small bay leaf
	Fresh ground pepper

METHOD

1. In saucepan combine all ingredients. Stir; add water if necessary to come up halfway on the celery. Cover pan and simmer for about 10 minutes. Celery should be tender but still crisp.
2. Remove from heat. Cool in the marinade.
3. Store in covered container until cold.
4. Garnish with lemon slices and fennel leaves if desired.

Balance with lower-fat dishes on days you use this recipe.

Fat Exchange 1	Saturated fat..................1 gram
Calories 75	Cholesterol.........0 milligrams
Carbohydrate ....3 grams	Fiber ....0.5 gram
Protein ....0 grams	Sodium.............55 milligrams
Fat ....7 grams (84%)	

VITAMIN SOUP

16 Servings/Serving size: 1 cup

Originally titled Hearty Barley Soup, this was dubbed Vitamin Soup by my family because all the liquid is from previous vegetable preparations. This can be stretched by adding another quart of broth, a little more barley, and any vegetables on hand such as zucchini, turnips, and cabbage. I make a canner full when the woodstove is going and freeze the soup in various size containers. The 1- or 2-cup size is just right for a shut-in; 4- or 6-cup for a family, and we use all sizes depending on who is around. Vitamin Soup tastes different each time it is made—maybe that's why we never tire of it.

INGREDIENTS

2	lb. soup bone that is 1/2 meat
3	qts. homemade vegetable broth
1/4	tsp. pepper
3	large parsley sprigs
1/3	cup barley
2	cups carrots, sliced
1	cup onion, diced
1	cup celery, sliced
4	cups tomatoes, fresh, canned, or frozen
2	cups peas, fresh or frozen

METHOD

1. Cut meat into cubes. Brown in fat cut from meat.
2. Add bone, broth, pepper, and parsley. Cook 1 hour.
3. Add barley. Cook 1 hour longer. Remove bone.
4. Add carrots, onion, celery, and tomatoes. Cook 30 minutes.
5. Add peas. Cook 15 minutes.

Vegetable Exchange	2	Fat	3 grams (26%)
Lean Meat Exchange	1	Saturated fat	1 gram
Calories	103	Cholesterol	19 milligrams
Protein	9 grams	Fiber	3 grams
Carbohydrates	10 grams	Sodium	272 milligrams

CHICKEN STOCK

This is a tasty, low-calorie stock for soups and sauces. Use the chicken and vegetables for salads, sandwiches, and casseroles. Freeze the broth in 1-cup portions. For alternatives to homemade stock, see page 3.

INGREDIENTS

3–3 1/2 lb. chicken pieces, backs and trimmings

1   stalk celery, sliced or a stalk of lovage from your herb garden

1   medium onion, chopped

1/2 leek, chopped, or large handful of fresh chives

1   small carrot, sliced

8–10 mushroom stems (optional)

1   tsp. peppercorns

2   bay leaves, crumbled

2   large sprigs fresh parsley

2   sprigs thyme or pinch of dried thyme

METHOD

1. Rinse chicken under cold running water.
2. Place all ingredients in a soup pot. Use enough water to almost cover food (about 3–4 qts.). Bring to a boil gradually. Simmer 40 minutes.
3. Turn off heat and let set for about 30 minutes. Strain into a bowl.
4. Cool broth and refrigerate.
5. Remove congealed fat. Use broth within three days or freeze.
6. Debone chicken and refrigerate. Especially good in the Pita Sandwich found in the CHICKEN AND TURKEY section.

Free Food	Saturated fat ....trace
Calories 7	Cholesterol.........................10 milligrams
Carbohydrate ....0 grams	Fiber...0 grams
Protein ....1.3 grams	Sodium.............................48 milligrams
Fat.................................0.5 grams (64%)	

TURKISH SPINACH SOUP

4 Servings/Serving size: 1 cup

Try this for a light first course for dinner or with a pita bread sandwich for lunch.

INGREDIENTS

1   small carrot, chopped
1   small stalk celery, chopped
1   small onion, chopped
3   cups chicken stock or 3 chick-
    en or vegetable bouillon cubes
    dissolved in 3 cups of water
8   oz. fresh spinach, chopped, or
    4 oz. frozen chopped spinach
2   Tbsp. whole-wheat pastry
    flour
    Juice of 1/2 lemon

METHOD

1. In a large saucepan, boil carrot, celery, and onion in stock 5 minutes.
2. Add spinach and simmer 5 minutes more. Remove from heat.
3. In a cup, mix together flour and lemon juice to make a thin, smooth paste, adding a little cold water if necessary.
4. Add 1/2 cup soup liquid and stir well.
5. Add flour mixture to soup and bring to a boil, stirring constantly.
6. Simmer for 2 minutes, then serve.

Vegetable Exchange 2
Calories 53
Carbohydrate ....8 grams
Protein ....3.6 grams
Fat...............................1 gram (17%)

Saturated fat ....trace
Cholesterol........................29 milligrams
Fiber.......................................2.4 grams
Sodium............................82 milligrams

NORWEGIAN SPINACH SOUP

4 Servings/Serving size: 1 cup

Light and wholesome, this Norwegian favorite is quick to prepare, low in calories, and high in taste appeal.

INGREDIENTS

8	oz. fresh spinach or frozen chopped spinach, partially thawed
4	cups homemade chicken stock
1	small onion, minced
1	Tbsp. reduced-calorie margarine
1	Tbsp. flour
	Pinch sugar (optional)
1/2	tsp. nutmeg, freshly grated
1/16	tsp. salt (optional)

METHOD

1. Wash, drain, and coarsely chop the fresh spinach.
2. In a medium saucepan, bring the stock with the onion to a boil. Stir in the spinach, lower the heat, and cook uncovered for 5 minutes. Remove from heat. Use the same burner for the next step.
3. Make a roux to thicken and flavor the soup: in a small saucepan, melt the margarine, add the flour, and stir over low heat for a few minutes without browning. Remove from heat and gradually add about 1 cup of the soup liquid, stirring constantly. When smooth, stir the mixture into the soup.
4. Return soup to the heat and slowly bring to a boil. Stir and cook until the soup thickens slightly. Season with a speck of sugar (if you like), nutmeg to suit your taste, and a pinch of salt.

Balance with lower-fat dishes on days you use this recipe.

Vegetable Exchange	1	Saturated fat .... trace
Calories	46	Cholesterol .... 39 milligrams
Carbohydrate	5 grams	Fiber .... 2 grams
Protein	2 grams	Sodium .... 142 milligrams
Fat	2 grams (39%)	Without added salt .... 106 milligrams

DIETER'S DELIGHT VEGETABLE SOUP

2 Servings/Serving size: 1 cup

INGREDIENTS

2 1/2	cups chicken broth*
1	tsp. lite soy sauce
1/8	tsp. thyme
1/8	tsp. basil
1/4	tsp. dried onion flakes
1/4	lb. fresh broccoli, cut into bite-size pieces
1	medium carrot, cut into 2 1/2 x 1/4-inch strips
1	cup lettuce, shredded

METHOD

1. Combine all ingredients except lettuce.
2. Boil gently 4–5 minutes or until vegetables are tender.
3. Stir in lettuce. Serve hot.

*Preferably homemade. See Chicken Stock directions (page 19) OR use 1 can (10 3/4 oz.) low-sodium condensed chicken broth and 1 can water OR use 3 packets of low-sodium chicken bouillon granules and 2 1/2 cups of water.

Vegetable Exchange	1	Saturated fat	trace
Calories	41	Cholesterol	39 milligrams
Carbohydrate	6 grams	Fiber	1 gram
Protein	2 grams	Sodium	90 milligrams
Fat	1 gram (22%)		

LENTIL SOUP*

12 Servings/Serving size: 1 cup

Make this when the wood stove is going or you need extra heat in the house. It is very good even without the grated cheese.

INGREDIENTS

2	Tbsp. olive oil	1 1/2	cups dried lentils, rinsed
2	large onions, chopped (2 cups)	1/2	tsp. salt (optional)
		1/4–1/2	tsp. black pepper
3	carrots, coarsely grated	1/3	cup dry white wine (optional)
3/4	tsp. marjoram	1/3	cup chopped fresh parsley or 2 Tbsp. dried parsley flakes
3/4	tsp. thyme leaves		
1	can (28 oz.) tomatoes with their juice	1/2	cup low-fat cheddar cheese or soy mozzarella, grated
7	cups broth: beef, chicken or vegetable		

METHOD

1. Heat the oil in a large saucepan, and saute the onions, carrots, marjoram, and thyme for about 5 minutes.
2. Add the tomatoes, broth, and lentils.
3. Bring to a boil, reduce the heat, cover the pan, and simmer the soup for about 1 hour or until the lentils are tender.
4. Add the salt, pepper, wine, and parsley and simmer the soup for a few minutes.
5. Serve with cheese sprinkled on each portion.

⚖ Balance with lower-fat dishes on days you use this recipe. *Not recommended for low-sodium diets if salt is added.

Lean Meat Exchange	1	Saturated fat	1 gram
Vegetable Exchange	2	Cholesterol	24 milligrams
Calories	95	Fiber	2 grams
Carbohydrate	12 grams	Sodium	399 milligrams
Protein	5 grams	Without added salt	304 milligrams
Fat	3 grams (28%)		

FRENCH ONION SOUP*

5 Servings/Serving size: 1 cup

INGREDIENTS

4–5	large onions, sliced
2	Tbsp. reduced-calorie margarine
1/4	tsp. sugar
1	Tbsp. flour
1/4	cup white wine
10	oz. low-sodium chicken broth
10	oz. low-sodium beef broth
1 1/2	cups water
5	slices French bread, toasted
4	oz. low-fat Swiss cheese, shredded
1/4	cup Parmesan cheese

METHOD

1. Combine onions and margarine in 3-qt. casserole. Cover.
2. Microwave 6–9 minutes on HIGH until onions are soft and translucent.
3. Stir in sugar, flour, wine, broth, and water. Cover. Microwave 4–6 minutes on HIGH or until heated through.
4. Ladle soup into individual casseroles. Top with bread slices. Sprinkle with cheeses. Microwave 5–7 minutes on MEDIUM-HIGH (70% power) or until cheeses melt.

*Not recommended for low-sodium diets.

Starch/Bread Exchange	1 1/2	Fat	7 grams (30%)
Lean Meat Exchange	1	Saturated fat	2.5 grams
Calories	208	Cholesterol	21 milligrams
Carbohydrate	24 grams	Fiber	2 grams
Protein	12 grams	Sodium	605 milligrams

BROCCOLI-CAULIFLOWER LUNCHEON SOUP

4–5 Servings/Serving size: 1 cup

INGREDIENTS

1   pkg. (10 oz.) frozen broccoli, chopped
1   pkg. (10 oz.) frozen cauliflower, chopped
1/3 cup onions, chopped
2   tsp. instant low-sodium chicken bouillon
1 1/2 cups water
1   Tbsp. cornstarch
14 oz. can evaporated skim milk, undiluted
1/4 tsp. salt (optional)
     Freshly ground pepper
1/4 tsp. nutmeg, freshly grated if possible
1/4 cup low-fat cheese, shredded

METHOD

1. Cook vegetables and bouillon in water for 5 minutes. Turn off heat and let stand for 15 minutes.
2. Puree in blender in two batches, about 3 pulses each batch.
3. Combine cornstarch and milk; add to vegetables. Use an additional 1/2 cup of water to rinse out milk can and blender. Add to soup.
4. Season with salt, pepper, and nutmeg.
5. Heat until bubbly. Do not boil.
6. Stir in cheese. Serve hot.

Skim Milk Exchange	1	Saturated fat	trace
Starch Exchange	1	Fiber	5 grams
Calories	153	Cholesterol	11 milligrams
Carbohydrate	23 grams	Sodium	429 milligrams
Protein	13 grams	Without added salt	285 milligrams
Fat	1 gram (6%)		

VEGETABLE CREAM SOUP*

4 Servings/Serving size: 1 cup

You can make this soup from scratch in 20 minutes while muffins are cooking. Use any vegetables that you have in abundance. I will give directions for cauliflower, because that was popular when I made it for microwave oven demonstrations. Other vegetables such as broccoli, asparagus, zucchini, tomatoes, or carrots can be substituted for cauliflower. Reduce or increase time as necessary so vegetables are almost tender.

INGREDIENTS

1	small head cauliflower
2	Tbsp. water
1	medium onion, chopped
2	Tbsp. reduced-calorie margarine
1/4	cup flour
1/2	tsp. salt (optional)
4	cups skim milk
4	oz. low-fat cheddar cheese, shredded
2	tsp. Dijon-style mustard

METHOD

1. Cut cauliflower in bite-size chunks; combine with water, onion, and margarine in a 3-qt. casserole.
2. Cover. Microwave 5–6 minutes on HIGH or until almost tender.
3. Combine flour, salt, and milk, mixing well. Stir into vegetables.
4. Cover. Microwave 10–12 minutes on HIGH or until mixture boils and thickens, stirring 2 or 3 times.
5. Stir in cheese and mustard. Microwave 2–3 minutes on HIGH or until cheese is melted, stirring once.

*Not recommended for low-sodium diets.

Medium-Fat Meat Exchange	1	Fat	6 grams (20%)
Vegetable Exchange	1	Saturated fat	2 grams
Skim Milk Exchange	1	Cholesterol	14 milligrams
Starch/Bread Exchange	1	Fiber	3 grams
Calories	266	Sodium	974 milligrams
Carbohydrate	32 grams	Without added salt	687 milligrams
Protein	21 grams		

CAULIFLOWER-CHEESE SOUP*

8 Servings/Serving size: 1 cup

Make this when cauliflower is flourishing in your garden or is a supermarket special. It is delicate and delicious and reheats well by the bowl in the microwave oven at 50% power or slowly in a heavy kettle or double boiler.

INGREDIENTS

2   cups potato chunks
3 1/2 cups cauliflowerets, divided
1   medium carrot, chopped
3   medium cloves garlic, sliced
1   large onion, chopped
1/2 tsp. salt (optional)
4   cups water or stock
1 1/2 cups low-fat cheddar cheese,
      grated
3/4 cup 1% low-fat milk
1/4 tsp. dill weed
1/4 tsp. caraway seed
1/4 tsp. dry mustard
      Black pepper
3/4 cup buttermilk
8   tsp. chopped scallions or
      chives

METHOD

1. Cook potatoes, 2 cups cauliflower, carrots, garlic, onion, salt, and water for 10 minutes.
2. Turn burner off and let set 15 minutes.
3. Puree in blender until smooth and creamy.
4. Heat gently and whisk in cheese, milk, and spices.
5. Steam or saute remaining cauliflower (use microwave if you have one) and add to soup.
6. Just before serving, whisk in buttermilk. Garnish with scallions.

*Not recommended for low-sodium diets if salt is added.

Milk Exchange 1	Saturated fat ....1.3 grams
Calories 106	Cholesterol......................24 milligrams
Carbohydrate ....13 grams	Fiber...................................2 grams
Protein ....9 grams	Sodium.........................527 milligrams
Fat.................................2 grams (17%)	Without added salt..........384 milligrams

CHICK PEA AND SPINACH SOUP*

6 Servings/Serving size: 1 cup

Serve this robust soup with one of the plain whole-wheat breads from the BREAD section of this book and finish the meal with a hearty cheesecake from the DESSERT section.

INGREDIENTS

1	large onion, chopped
2	cloves garlic, minced
2	Tbsp. olive oil
1	lb. can chick peas (garbanzo beans)
1	lb. fresh spinach, washed, tough stems removed, cut into 2-inch strips
2	Tbsp. parsley, chopped
1	Tbsp. paprika
1/4	tsp. pepper
1	bay leaf
6	cups fat-free vegetable or chicken broth
1/4	cup egg substitute or 1 egg Juice of 1 lemon

METHOD

1. Saute the onion and garlic in oil.
2. Add undrained chick peas, spinach, parsley, paprika, pepper, bay leaf, and broth. Combine well and simmer covered, over low heat for 10 minutes. Bring to boil.
3. Combine egg substitute, lemon juice, and 1/4 cup of soup broth.
4. Stir into boiling soup and remove from heat.

*Not recommended for low-sodium diets.

Starch/Bread Exchange	1 1/2	Saturated fat	1 gram
Medium-Fat Meat Exchange	1	Cholesterol	0 milligrams
Calories	203	with egg	36 milligrams
Carbohydrate	25 grams	Fiber	7 grams
Protein	10 grams	Sodium	414 milligrams
Fat	7 grams (28%)		

5 Servings/Serving size: 1 cup

For many years my husband and children came home for lunch every day. This chowder was a favorite meal. Back then, I used more margarine and evaporated whole milk. Now I use evaporated skim milk. For best flavor, let cool and reheat. Serve with bran muffins, a substantial salad, and dessert with fruit in it.

INGREDIENTS

1	large onion, sliced
2	Tbsp. margarine
2	medium unpeeled potatoes, cubed
1/4	tsp. salt (optional) and pepper
14	oz. evaporated skim milk, undiluted
1	lb. can cream-style corn

METHOD

1. Saute onion in margarine.
2. Add potatoes, salt, pepper, and enough water to barely cover. Cook until potatoes are soft.
3. Add milk and corn. Rinse out milk can with 1/4 cup additional water and add to chowder. Stir. Heat but do not boil.

*Not recommended for low-sodium diets if salt is added.

Starch/Bread Exchange 1	Fat....................5 grams (19%)
Fat Exchange 1	Saturated fat....................1 gram
Skim Milk Exchange.......................1	Cholesterol....................3 milligrams
Calories 241	Fiber....................0 milligrams
Protein......................10 grams	Sodium....................515 milligrams
Carbohydrates......................39 grams	Without added salt..........400 milligrams

FISH CHOWDER

8 Servings/Serving size: 1 cup

Corn muffins, carrot and celery sticks, and a fruit dessert or cookies from the DESSERT section will complete this meal. For variation, you can add a can of mixed vegetables with liquid when milk is added.

INGREDIENTS

2	large onions, sliced
3	Tbsp. reduced-calorie margarine
2	large potatoes, cut into 3/4-inch cubes (smooth Maine potatoes do not need to be peeled)
1/2	tsp. salt (optional)
1/8	tsp. pepper
1	lb. white fish, cut into 1 inch chunks
14	oz. can evaporated skim milk, undiluted

METHOD

1. Saute onions in margarine.
2. Add potatoes, salt, pepper, and enough water to nearly cover. Stir. Cook until potatoes are tender crisp.
3. Add fish and cook until vegetables are tender and fish flakes.
4. Add milk. Heat and serve. Chowder tastes even better if allowed to cool and then is reheated slowly.

Starch/Bread Exchange 1
Vegetable Exchange 1
Lean Meat Exchange.............................2
Calories 185
Protein ....16 grams
Carbohydrates...........................19 grams
Fat................................5 grams (24%)

Saturated fat ....0.88 grams
Cholesterol.........................26 milligrams
Fiber...2 grams
Sodium...........................307 milligrams
Without added salt..........164 milligrams

CREAMY BLUE CHEESE DRESSING

12 Servings/Serving size: 2 Tbsp.

Rich and creamy for salad greens or vegetable dips.

INGREDIENTS

1	cup nonfat cottage cheese
2	Tbsp. crumbled blue cheese
3	Tbsp. skim milk
1	clove garlic

METHOD

1. Place the cottage cheese, blue cheese, and milk in a blender or food processor.
2. Push the garlic through a garlic press into the work bowl. Process for about 20 seconds. (The blue cheese should still be chunky.)
3. Keeps for 1 week in a tightly covered jar in the refrigerator.

Lean Meat Exchange	1/2	Saturated fat	0.5 grams
Calories	25	Cholesterol	4 milligrams
Carbohydrate	2 grams	Fiber	0 grams
Protein	3 grams	Sodium	103 milligrams
Fat	0.5 gram (18%)		

GARDEN SALAD

2 Servings/Serving size: 1 cup

Here is a nice light salad that you can put together in a jiffy using olive oil cooking spray. This recipe may be doubled.

INGREDIENTS

1/2	head Boston lettuce
	Olive oil cooking spray
1/2	clove garlic
1/4	tsp. basil
1/8	tsp. salt (optional)
1/8	tsp. pepper
1	Tbsp. red wine vinegar
1	medium tomato, cut into wedges

METHOD

1. Wash lettuce; pat dry and cut or tear into bite-size pieces.
2. Spray a medium-size bowl with olive oil cooking spray, about 2 seconds. Rub bowl with 1/2 clove of garlic.
3. Put lettuce into bowl. Spray lettuce directly with olive oil cooking spray for about 4 seconds.
4. Add basil, salt, and pepper. Toss lettuce to combine.
5. Add vinegar. Toss well. Add tomato.

Vegetable Exchange................................1	Saturated fat................................0 grams
Calories..24	Cholesterol..........................0 milligrams
Carbohydrate...........................5 grams	Fiber...2 grams
Protein...1 gram	Sodium ....159 milligrams
Fat.......................................0 grams (0%)	Without added salt............15 milligrams

PERSIAN SALAD

6 Servings/Serving size: 1/6 recipe with 2 tsp. dressing

Add flavor treats from your herb garden to this crisp, raw salad.

INGREDIENTS

1	clove garlic, cut in half
1	head crisp lettuce (Romaine, Iceberg, etc.)
2	ripe tomatoes, sliced or quartered
3	scallions, finely sliced
3	radishes, finely sliced
1/2	cup fresh parsley, chopped
1/4	cup fresh dill, chopped
1/2	cup fresh mint, chopped

Lemon Dressing:

2	Tbsp. olive oil
1 1/2	Tbsp. lemon juice
1	clove garlic, crushed
1/8	tsp. salt (optional)
	Freshly ground pepper

METHOD

1. Rub a salad bowl with the cut garlic.
2. Wash the lettuce and dry thoroughly. Break into small pieces and drop in the salad bowl.
3. Add the tomatoes, onions, radishes, parsley, dill, and mint.
4. Mix all dressing ingredients and add to salad immediately or refrigerate and use later.
5. Toss with the dressing. Divide into 6 portions and serve.

⚖ Balance with lower-fat dishes on days you use this recipe.

Vegetable Exchange	1
Calories	24
Carbohydrate	4 grams
Protein	2 grams
Fat	0 grams (0%)
Saturated fat	0 grams
Cholesterol	0 milligrams
Fiber	2 grams
Sodium	30 milligrams

Lemon Dressing:

Fat Exchange	1
Calories	45
Carbohydrate	trace
Protein	trace
Fat	5 grams (100%)
Saturated fat	trace
Cholesterol	0 milligrams
Fiber	0 grams
Sodium	25 milligrams
Without added salt	trace

SPINACH-APPLE SALAD

6 Servings/Serving size: 1 1/4 cup

INGREDIENTS

10   oz. fresh spinach
1/2 lb. (2 large) tart apples such as Granny Smith, cored and sliced
1/4 cup corn or olive oil
1 1/2 Tbsp. wine vinegar
2   tsp. lite soy sauce
1/2 tsp. dry mustard
1/2 tsp. sugar
1   tsp. lemon juice
     Hot pepper sauce, such as Tabasco, to taste

METHOD

1. Remove tough spinach stems. Rinse leaves thoroughly and pat dry. Tear or cut into bite-size pieces.
2. Add apple slices.
3. Combine remaining ingredients. Toss with spinach and apple.
4. Serve in bowls.

Balance with lower-fat dishes on days you use this recipe.

Fat Exchange 2	Fat ....10 grams (60%)
Fruit Exchange 1	Saturated fat..................................1 gram
Calories 150	Cholesterol..........................0 milligrams
Carbohydrate ....13 grams	Fiber...4 grams
Protein......................................2 grams	Sodium............................38 milligrams

SPINACH, CHICK PEA, AND MUSHROOM SALAD

8 Servings/Serving size: 1 cup

INGREDIENTS

6	Tbsp. olive oil or vegetable oil
2	Tbsp. lemon juice
1/4	tsp. salt
1/4	tsp. pepper
1/4	tsp. dried or 2 Tbsp. fresh mint leaves
1	can (8 oz.) chick peas (garbanzo beans), drained
1/4	lb. fresh mushrooms, sliced
1	pkg.(10 oz.) fresh spinach, stems removed, leaves washed and patted dry

METHOD

1. Combine oil, lemon juice, salt, pepper, and mint in bottom of salad bowl; add chick peas, then top with mushroom slices and spinach.
2. Toss thoroughly so that all leaves are covered with the dressing.

⚖ Balance with lower-fat dishes on days you use this recipe.

Fat Exchange 2	Fat....................................11 grams (70%)
Vegetable Exchange..............................1	Saturated fat ....1.5 grams
Calories 141	Cholesterol..........................0 milligrams
Carbohydrate ....8 grams	Fiber..2.5 grams
Protein ....2.5 grams	Sodium..........................175 milligrams

EGGLESS TOFU MAYONNAISE

12 Servings/Serving size: 2 Tbsp.

Incredibly simple and delicious. It is loaded with calories, but no cholesterol. It is so rich that a little bit goes a long way. Some tasters liked it as a dip for fresh veggies. I prefer it mixed with low-fat cottage cheese and chives as a dip, or on fish, salad, fruit, and cold vegetables.

INGREDIENTS

1	cup (8 oz.) firm tofu, drained
1	Tbsp. Dijon mustard
3	Tbsp. lemon juice, divided
1/2	cup safflower oil
	Salt and pepper to taste

METHOD

1. In blender, place tofu, mustard, and half of the lemon juice. Blend until combined.
2. Very slowly, blend in oil and the rest of the lemon juice, drop by drop. Stop blender several times and scrape sides of jar with rubber scraper. The slower the ingredients are combined the thicker the mayonnaise will be.
3. Add salt and pepper to taste.
4. Cover and chill. Will keep at least two weeks.

⚖ Balance with lower-fat dishes on days you use this recipe.

Fat Exchange	2	Saturated fat	2 grams
Calories	115	Cholesterol	0 milligrams
Carbohydrate	1 gram	Fiber	trace
Protein	3 grams	Sodium	39 milligrams
Fat	11 gram (86%)		

HELLENIC VILLAGE SALAD

8 Servings/Serving size: 1 cup

This colorful raw salad might be your favorite whenever these vegetables are in season.

INGREDIENTS

4–5	ripe tomatoes, sliced
1	clove garlic, cut
1	large cucumber, diced
2	medium green bell peppers, seeded and sliced
3	scallions or 1 round onion, sliced
16	Greek olives, rinsed
2	oz. feta cheese, broken into small chunks
1	Tbsp. olive oil
2	Tbsp. vinegar
	Freshly ground pepper
	Dried oregano for garnish

METHOD

1. Place the tomatoes in a salad bowl that has been rubbed with the cut garlic.
2. Add the cucumber, peppers, onions, olives, and feta.
3. Sprinkle the olive oil, vinegar, and pepper over the salad. Stir thoroughly. Top with oregano.
4. Serve cold.

Balance with lower-fat dishes on days you use this recipe. *Not recommended for low-sodium diets.

Vegetable Exchange 2	Fat .... 7 grams (61%)
Fat Exchange 1	Saturated fat ....2 grams
Calories 103	Cholesterol..........................6 milligrams
Carbohydrate ....7 grams	Fiber...2 grams
Protein ....3 grams	Sodium...........................414 milligrams

CHINESE SPROUT SALAD

2 Servings/Serving size: 1/2 cup

This salad is a great use for bean sprouts. To make your own sprouts: Rinse a small handful of mung beans in a jar; cover with cheesecloth; place jar on its side; rinse beans 2–3 times daily and drain off all the water. The beans will sprout in a few days and triple in volume. Store in the refrigerator and use within a few days.

INGREDIENTS

1	tsp. peanut oil
5–6	peppercorns
1–2	Tbsp. white wine vinegar
1/2	tsp. sugar (optional)
2	tsp. lite soy sauce
1	cup fresh bean sprouts
1	scallion, including green part, thinly sliced
8	small tender lettuce leaves

METHOD

1. Heat the oil in a very small pan and add the peppercorns. Cook gently for a few minutes.
2. Add the vinegar, sugar (if you are using it), and soy sauce. Stir thoroughly. Remove the peppercorns.
3. Pour sauce over the sprouts. Add the scallion, and toss to mix thoroughly.
4. Serve cold on lettuce.

⚖ Balance with lower-fat dishes on days you use this recipe.

Vegetable Exchange 1	Fat ....3 grams (40%)
Fat Exchange 1/2	Saturated fat ....trace
Calories 67	Cholesterol.........................0 milligrams
Carbohydrate ....7 grams	Fiber..4 grams
Protein ....3 grams	Sodium ....36 milligrams

CARROT SALAD

9 Servings/Serving size: 1/3 cup

You won't even miss the usual oil dressing.

INGREDIENTS

2	cups carrot, shredded
1/4	cup raisins
1	small apple, sliced
1	cup cantaloupe or other melon, sliced
3	Tbsp. orange juice
24	Lettuce leaves

METHOD

1. Combine all ingredients except lettuce.
2. Refrigerate for a few hours until the raisins absorb the juice.
3. Divide into 9 parts on salad plates lined with crisp lettuce.
4. Serve cold.

Fruit Exchange 1	Saturated fat ....trace
Calories 53	Cholesterol.........................0 milligrams
Carbohydrate ....12 grams	Fiber...3 grams
Protein ....1.3 grams	Sodium.............................17 milligrams
Fat......................................0 grams (0%)	

COUSCOUS SPINACH SALAD

8 Servings/Serving size: 1 cup

A delightful dish for a summer barbecue. Make this instead of a macaroni salad for a change. With just six ingredients it goes together quickly. Couscous is finely cracked wheat that has been steamed, dried, and refined to some extent. It may be found on the rice or hot cereal shelves of supermarkets and in health food stores.

INGREDIENTS

1	cup chicken broth
3/4	cup couscous
1/2	cup low-calorie Italian salad dressing
2	cups fresh spinach, shredded
12	cherry tomatoes, halved
1	can (8 oz.) water chestnuts, sliced
1	cup fresh spinach leaves

METHOD

1. In a saucepan, bring chicken broth to boiling. Stir in couscous.
2. Remove from heat. Cover. Let stand for 5 minutes.
3. Add salad dressing. Cover and chill.
4. To serve, toss couscous mixture with shredded spinach, tomatoes, and water chestnuts.
5. Serve on spinach leaves.

Fat Exchange	1/2	Fat	3 grams (19%)
Starch/Bread Exchange	1	Saturated fat	trace
Vegetable Exchange	1	Cholesterol	5 milligrams
Calories	139	Fiber	6 grams
Carbohydrate	24 grams	Sodium	275 milligrams
Protein	4 grams		

BLUEBERRY SALAD MOLD

8 Servings/Serving size: 1/2 cup

This is lovely served on tender lettuce leaves and decorated with a wreath of fresh fruit such as melon balls. Suitable for a light lunch, an elegant buffet, or a spectacular dessert (minus the lettuce).

INGREDIENTS

1	can (15 oz.) blueberries packed in water without sugar
1	pkg. (3 oz.) lemon gelatin, regular or sugar-free
1	cup boiling hot water
1	cup nonfat ricotta cheese
1/4	cup chopped walnuts

METHOD

1. Drain blueberries. Save juice; add enough cold water to make 3/4 cup.
2. Dissolve gelatin in the 1 cup of hot water, add blueberry juice. Refrigerate until partially set.
3. Mix the blueberries and one half of the gelatin mixture and pour into a salad mold. Refrigerate.
4. Whip remaining gelatin until fluffy, add cheese, and beat until smooth. Stir in nuts.
5. Spread whipped gelatin mix over blueberry layer.
6. Chill until firm.

Based on sugar-free gelatin:

Lean Meat Exchange	1	Fat	2 grams (27%)
Fruit Exchange	1/2	Saturated fat	trace
Calories	66	Cholesterol	0 milligrams
Carbohydrate	7 grams	Fiber	2 grams
Protein	5 grams	Sodium	10 milligrams

PASTA SALAD*

6 Servings/Serving size: 1 cup

Use any shape of pasta you like. I used three-color spirals, colored with tomato, beet, and spinach powder, right off the supermarket shelf. Made in the morning, we had this salad with grilled fish on the first night out on a camping trip. Because refrigeration was available, we enjoyed the leftovers the next noon—instant lunch while everyone else was making sandwiches.

INGREDIENTS

3	cups cooked tricolor spiral pasta (1 1/2 cups dry)
1	large, ripe tomato, chopped
1	medium green pepper, chopped
1	cup low-fat cheese, shredded
1	cup black olives, drained and sliced
6	Tbsp. bottled low-calorie Italian dressing
16	tender lettuce leaves

METHOD

1. Cook pasta the energy saving way by boiling water and adding pasta as usual. Stir until water boils again. Cover. Turn off heat. Let stand for the cooking time indicated on the package.
2. Drain.
3. Add rest of ingredients except lettuce and chill.
4. Serve on lettuce.

⚖ Balance with lower-fat dishes on days you use this recipe. *Not recommended for low-sodium diets.

Starch/Bread Exchange	1	Protein	10 grams
Fat Exchange	1	Fat	7 grams (31%)
Meat Exchange	1	Saturated fat	2 grams
Vegetable Exchange	1	Cholesterol	7 milligrams
Calories	203	Fiber	4 grams
Carbohydrate	25 grams	Sodium	636 milligrams

QUINOA-VEGETABLE SALAD

8 Servings/Serving size: 1 cup

Quinoa (pronounced keen-wa) is a natural whole grain containing high quality protein and iron. It is available in health food stores and some supermarkets. If you can't find it, substitute 6 ounces of couscous or bulgar wheat; follow label directions for cooking. Take this to the next pot luck supper you attend. It will be a welcome change from the usual pasta.

INGREDIENTS

1	cup quinoa or bulgar	1/2	cup carrot, chopped
2	cups chicken stock or water	1/2	cup sliced scallions
2	ripe tomatoes, chopped	1	clove garlic, minced
2	cups cucumber, chopped	1/2	cup lemon juice
1	cup celery, chopped	1	Tbsp. plus 1 tsp. olive oil
1	cup packed parsley, chopped	1/4	tsp. salt (optional)
1	cup packed fresh mint leaves, chopped		

METHOD

1. Rinse grain in medium strainer; drain. Place in 2-qt. saucepan with chicken stock or water and bring to boil. Reduce heat and simmer, covered, for 10–15 minutes, or until all water is absorbed.
2. Transfer grain to large bowl.
3. Add tomatoes, cucumber, celery, parsley, mint, carrots, scallions, and garlic.
4. Sprinkle lemon juice, olive oil, and salt over salad. Mix to combine flavors.
5. Chill 1 hour before serving.

Starch/Bread Exchange 1	Fat ....3 grams (21%)
Vegetable Exchange 1	Saturated fat ....trace
Fat Exchange 1/2	Cholesterol..........................10 milligrams
Calories 127	Fiber...4 grams
Carbohydrate ....21 grams	Sodium............................121 milligrams
Protein ....4 grams	Without added salt............49 milligrams

VERY-LOW-CALORIE TOMATO DRESSING

6 Servings/Serving size: 1/4 cup

This dressing is nice on plain lettuce, tossed salads, and chef's salads.

INGREDIENTS

1	can (6 oz.) tomato or V-8 juice
1/4	cup vinegar
2	Tbsp. vegetable oil (olive oil gives a robust flavor)
1	Tbsp. lemon juice
1	Tbsp. Dijon mustard
1	Tbsp. chopped fresh chives
1	Tbsp. minced fresh parsley
1	large clove garlic, minced
1/2	tsp. dried or 1 Tbsp. fresh basil
1/8	tsp. cayenne or to taste

METHOD

1. Combine all ingredients in a jar. Shake well to blend.
2. Refrigerate. Shake before each use.

Vegetable Exchange 1
Calories 25
Carbohydrate .... 3 grams
Protein .... 1 gram
Fat .... 1 gram (36%)

Saturated fat .... trace
Cholesterol .... 0 milligrams
Fiber .... trace
Sodium .... 94 milligrams

BREAD-MAKING TIPS

Smaller loaves cook faster than large loaves, saving both time and energy.

When possible bake two or three loaves at the same time. More energy is needed to bake one loaf at a time.

Many breads can be baked as a part of an oven meal.

Take care not to overbake muffins or they will be dry and hard. They usually start to pull away from the sides of the cups when done. Or use a toothpick or cake tester to determine when they are fully baked.

Most breads made without yeast can be cooked as muffins in about one-half the time it takes to bake a loaf.

When making quick breads and desserts, you will have better results if all dry ingredients that will go through the sifter are sifted together. That includes dry milk granules, as well as the usual flours, leavening agents, spices, etc. Add the water for the dry milk to other liquids in the recipe.

Most of the muffins and breads in this collection are dense and chewy, not light and crumbly. Enjoy them warm from the oven.

Spray pans with nonstick vegetable cooking spray. There are several varieties available.

Yeast dough can be raised (proofed) in the microwave oven as follows:

Step 1. Microwave 3 cups of water in a 1-qt. measure on HIGH (100% power) for 2–3 minutes until steaming hot.

Step 2. Place bowl of dough in oven next to water. Cover bowl lightly with thin towel. Microwave at WARM (10% power) for 20–24 minutes.

Step 3. Test for raising by making an indentation with fingers; dough should not spring back, and surface should be dry. Shape bread and bake as recipe directs.

Unlike yeast-leavened baked goods, muffins are raised with baking powder and/or baking soda, both of which contain quite a bit of sodium. Low-sodium baking powder can be purchased in some health food stores and in special diet sections of supermarkets and can be used in place of double-acting baking powder. I have yet to find low-sodium baking soda. Baking soda is needed when a recipe contains acidic ingredients such as buttermilk or citrus juice.

Note: The BREAD section is large because the ingredients in breads are such an important part of a healthy diet.

DUTCH APPLE PANCAKES

12 Servings/Serving size: 2 small pancakes

Steaming hot and fragrant with apple, these are delicious for breakfast or brunch. Use any topping in the DESSERT section.

INGREDIENTS

1/2	Tbsp. (1/2 pkg.) active dry yeast
1/4	tsp. sugar
2	cups flour
1/4	tsp. salt (optional)
1 1/2	cups milk, warmed
1 1/4	tsp. reduced-calorie margarine or nonstick vegetable cooking spray
3	small apples, cored, peeled, and sliced (8 circles per apple)

METHOD

1. Dissolve the yeast and sugar in 1/2 cup warm water. Cover and set aside until doubled in bulk.
2. In a large bowl, mix the flour and salt. Make a well in the middle. Pour in the swollen yeast and add 1 1/4 cups milk to the well. Mix with a wooden spoon, adding only enough of the remaining milk to make a fairly thick batter.
3. Set aside in a warm place for about 30 minutes until bubbles begin to appear.
4. Melt 1/2 tsp. margarine on griddle or spray it with nonstick vegetable cooking spray. Pour 1/2 cup of batter on griddle. Place 4 or 5 slices of apple on the top (uncooked side).
5. When pancake bottom turns brown, turn over and brown the apple side. Be sure pancakes are cooked; they bake more slowly than baking powder pancakes.
6. Serve immediately with 1/2 tsp. margarine for each pancake or other topping of your choice.

Starch/Bread Exchange 1 1/2	Saturated fat (with margarine) ....trace
Calories 105	Cholesterol ....1 milligram
Carbohydrate ....21 grams	Fiber ....1 gram
Protein ....2 grams	Sodium...........................40 milligrams
Fat (with margarine) ....1 gram (9%)	Without added salt...........20 milligrams

APPLESAUCE MUFFINS

12 Servings/Serving size: 1 muffin

Applesauce makes the muffins tender and moist without overloading them with fat.

INGREDIENTS

1 1/4 cups unsweetened applesauce
1/4   cup egg substitute or 1 egg
2   Tbsp. canola oil
1/4   cup honey
1   cup whole-wheat flour
1   cup flour
2   tsp. baking powder
3/4   tsp. baking soda
1/2   tsp. cinnamon
1/4   tsp. nutmeg
1/3   cup raisins

METHOD

1. In a large bowl, beat together the applesauce, egg substitute, oil, and honey.
2. Sift in the dry ingredients, stirring just to moisten.
3. Stir in the raisins and divide the batter among 12 muffin cups coated with nonstick vegetable cooking spray.
4. Bake at 375° for 20 minutes.

Starch/Bread Exchange	1	Fat	3 grams (19%)
Fruit Exchange	1	Saturated fat	trace
Fat Exchange	1/2	Cholesterol	0 milligrams
Calories	143	with egg	18 milligrams
Carbohydrate	26 grams	Fiber	2 grams
Protein	3 grams	Sodium	130 milligrams

OATMEAL CARROT MUFFINS*

12 Servings/Serving size: 1 muffin

INGREDIENTS

1	cup buttermilk (dry mix or fresh)
1	cup rolled oats
1/2	cup carrots, grated
1/4	cup brown sugar
1/4	cup reduced-calorie corn-oil margarine
1/4	cup egg substitute
1	cup flour
1/4	cup sugar (artificial sweetener, if desired)
1	Tbsp. baking powder
1/2	tsp. salt (optional)
1/2	tsp. baking soda
1/2	cup raisins

METHOD

1. In large bowl, pour buttermilk over oats; stir to mix. Cover and let stand for 2 hours or refrigerate overnight.
2. Cream together brown sugar, margarine, and egg; stir into oat mixture and add carrots.
3. Sift together flour, sugar, baking powder, salt, and baking soda. Stir into batter just until moistened, then add raisins.
4. Spoon into muffin cups coated with nonstick vegetable cooking spray, filling almost to top. Bake at 400° for 20–25 minutes.
5. Let stand 2 minutes before removing from cups.

*For occasional use only, due to sugar content, if sugar is used.

With 1/4 cup sugar:

Starch/Bread Exchange	1
Fruit Exchange	1
Fat Exchange	1/2
Calories	151
Carbohydrate	27 grams
Protein	4 grams
Fat	3 grams (18%)
Saturated fat	1 gram
Cholesterol	1 milligram
Fiber	1 gram
Sodium	309 milligrams
Without added salt	213 milligrams

YOGURT-OATMEAL MUFFINS

12 Servings/Serving size: 1 muffin

Yogurt is the secret ingredient that makes this muffin moist and tender.

INGREDIENTS

1	cup quick-cooking rolled oats, not instant
1	cup low-fat plain yogurt
1/4	cup reduced-calorie margarine
2	Tbsp. dark brown sugar
1	small banana, mashed or 1/4 cup apple juice concentrate
1/4	cup egg substitute
1	cup flour
1/8	tsp. salt (optional)
1	tsp. baking powder
1/2	tsp. baking soda
1/2	cup raisins

METHOD

1. Mix the yogurt with the oatmeal and let stand 1 hour.
2. Cream margarine with sugar and banana or apple juice.
3. Add egg and oatmeal mixture.
4. Sift the dry ingredients into the oatmeal mixture. Stir in raisins.
5. Spoon into 12 muffin cups coated with nonstick vegetable cooking spray.
6. Bake at 375° for 20–25 minutes.

Starch/Bread Exchange	1	Fat	3 grams (19%)
Fruit Exchange	1	Saturated fat	1 gram
Fat Exchange	1/2	Cholesterol	1 milligram
Calories	139	Fiber	1 gram
Carbohydrate	22 grams	Sodium	155 milligrams
Protein	4 grams	Without added salt	131 milligrams

OAT BRAN/BANANA MUFFINS

12 Servings/Serving size: 1 muffin

This originally called for 1/2 cup sugar but I made it with 1/4 cup to go with coffee at a sewing club. We agreed it was lovely as a coffee cake but too sweet for a breakfast or luncheon bread. Another test with 2 tablespoons of sugar was just right.

INGREDIENTS

1/4	cup egg substitute
1/4	cup vegetable oil
2	Tbsp. granulated sugar
1	cup bananas, mashed
1	tsp. vanilla
1	cup whole-wheat flour
1	tsp. baking powder
1	tsp. baking soda
3/4	cup oat bran
1/2	cup raisins

METHOD

1. In bowl, combine egg substitute, oil, sugar, bananas, and vanilla; mix well.
2. In another bowl, mix together flour, baking soda, baking powder, oat bran, and raisins; stir into egg mixture, mixing only until combined.
3. Spoon into 12 muffin cups coated with nonstick vegetable cooking spray, filling each about 2/3 full.
4. Bake at 400° for 20–25 minutes or until firm to the touch. Remove from oven and let stand 2 minutes before removing muffins from cups.

⚖ Balance with lower-fat dishes on days you use this recipe.

Starch/Bread Exchange	1	Fat	5 grams (35%)
Fat Exchange	1	Saturated fat	trace
Calories	129	Cholesterol	0 milligrams
Carbohydrate	19 grams	Fiber	3 grams
Protein	3 grams	Sodium	115 milligrams

BUTTERMILK, BRAN, AND BLUEBERRY MUFFINS

20 Servings/Serving size: 1 muffin

Makes delicious and healthful low-fat, high-fiber muffins.

INGREDIENTS

1	cup wheat bran
1	cup oat bran
2	cups whole-wheat flour
1/3	cup granulated sugar
1	Tbsp. baking powder
1	tsp. baking soda
4	egg whites
2	cups buttermilk or sour milk
1/3	cup corn oil
1/3	cup molasses
1	cup fresh or frozen blueberries

METHOD

1. In large bowl, mix together bran, flour, sugar, baking powder, and baking soda.
2. In another bowl, combine egg whites, buttermilk, oil, and molasses; pour into bran mixture and stir just enough to moisten, being care ful not to overmix.
3. Fold in blueberries.
4. Spoon into muffin cups coated with nonstick vegetable cooking spray, filling almost to top.
5. Bake in 375° oven for 25 minutes or until firm to the touch. Remove from the oven and let stand for 2 minutes before removing muffins from cups.

Starch/Bread Exchange	1	Fat	5 grams (30%)
Fruit Exchange	1	Saturated fat	trace
Fat Exchange	1	Cholesterol	1 milligram
Calories	149	Fiber	4 grams
Carbohydrate	21 grams	Sodium	144 milligrams
Protein	5 grams		

MAINE BLUEBERRY MUFFINS

12 Servings/Serving size: 1 muffin

Use fresh or frozen Maine blueberries—a delightful way to stretch one cup of blueberries into twelve servings. But most people will want more than one muffin, especially when they are warm.

INGREDIENTS

1 3/4 cups plus 2 tsp. flour
1   cup blueberries, picked over and rinsed
1   Tbsp. baking powder
1/4 tsp. nutmeg
1/4 tsp. cinnamon
2   eggs or 1/2 cup egg substitute
1/4 cup vegetable oil
3/4 cup orange juice
1   tsp. lemon or orange rind, grated

METHOD

1. Lightly coat the blueberries with the 2 tsp. flour. (You can shake the flour and berries together in a paper bag.)
2. In a large bowl, mix together the 1 3/4 cups flour, baking powder, nutmeg, and cinnamon.
3. In a small bowl, beat the eggs or egg substitute lightly. Add oil, orange juice, and grated rind.
4. Add the liquid to dry mixture, and stir a few times gently.
5. Before the two mixtures are fully combined, add berries and lemon rind.
6. Spoon into muffin cups coated with nonstick vegetable spray, filling each cup about two-thirds full.
7. Bake at 400° 20–25 minutes.

⚖ Balance with lower-fat dishes on days you use this recipe..

Starch/Bread Exchange	1	Saturated fat	1 gram
Fat Exchange	1	Cholesterol	45 milligrams
Calories	140	with egg substitute	0 milligrams
Carbohydrate	19 grams	Fiber	1 gram
Protein	3 grams	Sodium	95 milligrams
Fat	6 grams (37%)	with egg substitute	106 milligrams

ZUCCHINI BREAD OR MUFFINS

12 Servings/Serving size: 1 muffin or 1 slice of bread

INGREDIENTS

1/2	cup raisins
1/4	cup apple juice concentrate
1/4	cup egg substitute
1/4	cup corn oil
1	ripe banana, sliced
1	tsp. vanilla
1	cup whole-wheat flour
1/2	cup flour
1/2	tsp. baking powder
1/2	tsp. baking soda
1	cup zucchini, fresh or frozen, shredded

METHOD

1. Heat raisins in apple juice until raisins are soft, about 3 minutes. (Takes about a minute in the microwave.)
2. Pour raisins and juice into blender and puree.
3. Add egg substitute, oil, banana, and vanilla and blend.
4. Sift dry ingredients into a large bowl.
5. Stir in blender ingredients and zucchini.
6. Spray a loaf pan or 12 muffin cups with nonstick vegetable spray. Spoon in batter.
7. Bake at 350° for about 50 minutes for loaf or 25 minutes for muffins.

⚖ Balance with lower-fat dishes on days you use this recipe.

Starch/Bread Exchange	1
Fat Exchange	1
Calories	129
Carbohydrate	19 grams
Protein	3 grams

Fat	5 grams (35%)
Saturated fat	1 gram
Cholesterol	0 milligrams
Fiber	2 grams
Sodium	64 milligrams

CARROT BREAD OR MUFFINS

12 Servings/Serving size: 1 muffin

INGREDIENTS

1	cup whole-wheat flour
1	tsp. baking powder
1/2	tsp. baking soda
2	tsp. cinnamon
1/4	tsp. salt (optional)
1/2	cup raisins
3	Tbsp. apple juice concentrate
1/4	cup egg substitute
1/4	cup vegetable oil
1	tsp. vanilla
1	ripe banana, sliced
1	cup raw carrots, grated

METHOD

1. Sift together dry ingredients.
2. Heat raisins in apple juice until raisins are soft and puffy. (Takes about a minute in the microwave oven).
3. Puree raisins with juice in blender.
4. Add egg, oil, vanilla, and banana. Blend.
5. Add to dry ingredients and stir lightly. Fold in carrots.
6. Spray a loaf pan or 12 muffin cups with nonstick vegetable cooking spray. Spoon in batter.
7. Bake at 350° about 45 minutes for loaf or about 25 minutes for muffins.
8. After cooling, cut loaf into 12 slices.

⚖ Balance with lower-fat dishes on days you use this recipe.

Starch/Bread Exchange	1	Saturated fat	trace
Fat Exchange	1	Cholesterol	0 milligrams
Calories	117	Fiber	2 grams
Carbohydrate	16 grams	Sodium	132 milligrams
Protein	2 grams	Without added salt	84 milligrams
Fat	5 grams (38%)		

WHOLE-WHEAT AND FRUIT BREAD OR MUFFINS

12 Servings/Serving size: 1 slice or 1 muffin

Sweetened naturally with three kinds of fruit. Hint: Keep a can of frozen apple juice concentrate on hand in the freezer and scoop out what you need for a recipe like this. Cover the top of the can with foil held by an elastic band.

INGREDIENTS

1/2	cup raisins
1/4	cup apple juice concentrate
1/4	cup egg substitute
1/4	cup corn oil
1	ripe banana, sliced
1	tsp. vanilla
1	cup whole-wheat flour
2	tsp. cinnamon
1/2	tsp. baking powder
1/2	tsp. baking soda
1/4	tsp. salt (optional)
1/4	cup chopped nuts, optional

METHOD

1. Heat raisins in apple juice for 3 minutes over high heat or 1 minute in the microwave oven.
2. Pour into blender and puree.
3. Add egg substitute, oil, banana, and vanilla and blend.
4. Mix dry ingredients in a bowl and add blender ingredients. Stir lightly.
5. Add nuts if you are using them.
6. Spoon into loaf pan or muffin cups coated with nonstick vegetable cooking spray. Bake at 350° 40–50 minutes for a loaf or 20–25 minutes for muffins.
7. After cooling, cut loaf into 12 slices.

Starch/Bread Exchange	1
Fat Exchange	1/2
Calories	99
Carbohydrate	16 grams
Protein	2 grams
Fat	3 grams (27%)
Saturated fat	trace
Cholesterol	0 milligrams
Fiber	2 grams
Sodium	129 milligrams
Without added salt	81 milligrams

NATURALLY SWEETENED DATE BREAD

15 Servings/Serving size: 1 slice

A high-fiber nutritious snack without added fat or cholesterol. Perfect for breakfast, lunch, and after school. Energy-saving tip: Double the recipe and bake two loaves at the same time.

INGREDIENTS

1	cup pitted dates (not sugared), snipped into pieces
1	cup raisins
1 1/2	cups boiling water
2	cups whole-wheat flour
1	tsp. baking soda
1	tsp. baking powder or 2 tsp. low-sodium baking powder
1/4	tsp. salt (optional)
2	egg whites, slightly beaten, fresh, reconstituted, or dried
1	tsp. vanilla
1/4–1/2	cup almonds, chopped or sliced

METHOD

1. Combine dates and raisins. Pour boiling water over mixture and cool slightly.
2. Sift flour, baking powder, baking soda, and salt into mixing bowl.
3. Stir egg whites and vanilla into cooled date mixture.
4. Add date mixture and almonds to flour mixture; stir until well blended. (Mixture will be thick.)
5. Spread in loaf pan coated with nonstick vegetable cooking spray.
6. Bake at 350° for 40–50 minutes or until a wooden toothpick inserted in center comes out clean. Cool in pan 10 minutes.
7. Remove from pan; cool on wire rack. Cut into 15 slices.

Starch/Bread Exchange	1	Fat	3 grams (16%)
Fruit Exchange	1	Saturated fat	trace
Fat Exchange	1/2	Cholesterol	0 milligrams
Calories	143	Fiber	4 grams
Carbohydrate	28 grams	Sodium	132 milligrams
Protein	4 grams	Without added salt	94 milligrams

APPLE-OAT BREAD

18 Servings/Serving size: 1 slice

Low in saturated fat and high in fiber, this loaf is a healthy choice for anytime of the day.

INGREDIENTS

1 1/2 cups uncooked rolled oats
1 1/2 cups flour
1 1/2 tsp. baking soda
1 1/2 tsp. cinnamon
3/4   tsp. allspice
1/2   cup honey
1/2   cup skim milk
1/4   cup corn oil
3   egg whites, fresh or dried
3   (1 1/4 lb.) cooking apples, diced

METHOD

1. In a large bowl, mix oats, flour, baking soda, cinnamon, and allspice.
2. In a small bowl, beat honey, milk, oil, and egg whites. Stir into flour mixture just until moistened.
3. Fold in apples.
4. Spread in loaf pan coated with nonstick vegetable cooking spray.
5. Bake at 350° for about 65 minutes.
6. Cool in pan on wire rack for 10 minutes and remove bread from pan. Finish cooling on wire rack. Cut into 18 slices.

Starch/Bread Exchange	1	Fat	4 grams (25%)
Fruit Exchange	1	Saturated fat	0.5 grams
Fat Exchange	1	Cholesterol	0 milligrams
Calories	144	Fiber	1 gram
Carbohydrate	24 grams	Sodium	82 milligrams
Protein	3 grams		

APPLESAUCE-OAT BREAD

18 Servings/Serving size: 1 slice

INGREDIENTS

1	cup whole-wheat flour
1	cup flour
1	cup rolled oats
4	tsp. baking powder
1	tsp. cinnamon
1/2	tsp. ground ginger
1/4	tsp. ground cloves
1/4	tsp. baking soda
1/4	tsp. salt (optional)
1	egg or 1/4 cup egg substitute
1/2	cup brown sugar
1 1/2 cups applesauce, unsweetened	
2	Tbsp. corn oil
1/3	cup raisins

METHOD

1. In a large bowl, combine the flours, oats, baking powder, cinnamon, ginger, cloves, baking soda, and salt.
2. In a medium bowl, beat together the egg, brown sugar, applesauce, and oil until they are well blended. Stir in raisins.
3. Combine mixtures, stirring ingredients just to moisten them. Pour into 9 x 5 x 3-inch loaf pan coated with nonstick vegetable cooking spray.
4. Bake the bread at 350° for 50–60 minutes or until a toothpick inserted in the center of the loaf comes out clean. Let the bread cool in the pan for 10 minutes and then turn out onto a wire rack to cool.
5. Cut into 18 slices.

Starch/Bread Exchange 1	Saturated fat ....trace
Fruit Exchange 1	Fiber ....1 gram
Calories 122	Cholesterol.........................12 milligrams
Carbohydrate ....23 grams	with egg substitute ....0 milligrams
Protein.......................................3 grams	Sodium............................145 milligrams
Fat.....................................2 grams (15%)	Without added salt............97 milligrams

WHOLE-WHEAT AND BRAN BREAD

20 Servings/Serving size: 1 slice

A wonderful quick and chewy round loaf of bread. Taste-testers liked it warm and crusty from the oven as well as toasted the next day.

INGREDIENTS

2	cups whole-wheat flour
1	cup bran
1	tsp. baking soda
1	tsp. cream of tartar
1/2	tsp. salt (optional)
1 1/4	cups buttermilk or whey from making yogurt cheese (see page 1)
1	Tbsp. corn oil

METHOD

1. Spray round baking dish with nonstick vegetable cooking spray.
2. In a large bowl, mix the flour, bran, baking soda, cream of tartar, and salt.
3. Make a well in the middle and pour in the buttermilk and oil. Mix quickly with a rubber scraper until flour disappears, folding dough with a kneading motion.
4. Shape a round loaf slightly domed in the middle, about 6 1/2 inches in diameter. Place in baking dish. With a knife, cut a cross on top from one side of the loaf to the other (to help prevent bread from cracking).
5. Bake at 425° for 25 minutes. Lower the heat to 350° for 10 minutes longer or turn heat off and finish cooking on heat stored in oven. Bread is done if it sounds hollow when tapped.

Starch/Bread Exchange	1	Saturated fat	trace
Calories	65	Cholesterol	1 milligram
Carbohydrate	11 grams	Fiber	2 grams
Protein	3 grams	Sodium	115 milligrams
Fat	1 gram (14%)	Without added salt	58 milligrams

WHOLE-WHEAT BANANA BREAD

24 Servings/Serving size: 1 slice

Try this when you have a lot of very ripe bananas on hand. Sometimes I use one loaf pan that's a little longer and make six muffins, too. The muffins cook in 20 minutes. Warm from the oven they taste like dessert.

INGREDIENTS

2	Tbsp. honey
3	Tbsp. vegetable oil
1	tsp. vanilla
2	cups (4 medium) bananas, mashed
2	Tbsp. lemon juice
2	cups whole-wheat flour
2	tsp. baking powder
1/2	tsp. baking soda
1/2	cup raisins
1/2	cup walnuts, chopped, or 1/2 cup Grape-Nuts

METHOD

1. Mix honey, oil, and vanilla.
2. Add bananas and lemon juice. Mix well.
3. Sift flour, baking powder, and baking soda into banana mixture. Stir.
4. Fold in raisins and nuts.
5. Bake in 2 loaf pans each 7 1/2 x 3 3/4 x 2 1/4 inches at 350° for 35–40 minutes (325° for black pans).
6. Cut each loaf into 12 slices.

Starch/Bread Exchange 1
Fat Exchange 1
Calories 108
   with Grape-Nuts 102
Carbohydrate ....16 grams
   with Grape-Nuts ....19 grams
Protein ....2 grams

Fat ....4 grams (33%)
   with Grape-Nuts ....2 grams (18%)
Saturated fat ....trace
Fiber...2 grams
Cholesterol..........................0 milligrams
Sodium................................86 milligrams

WHOLE-WHEAT BREAD

20 Servings/Serving size: 1 slice

Bread may be sweetened with fructose, a natural fruit sugar. Fructose causes less of a rise in blood glucose levels than other sugars and thus may be of particular interest to people with type II diabetes. Fructose has the same number of calories per gram as other sugars. Testers rated this bread superb when made with fructose and whey.

INGREDIENTS

2	cups whole-wheat flour
1	cup wheat bran
1	Tbsp. baking powder
1/4	tsp. baking soda
3	Tbsp. fructose or granulated sugar
1	tsp. cinnamon
1/3	cup raisins
2	cups whey from making yogurt cheese (see page 1) or 2 cups buttermilk
1	egg
1	Tbsp. vanilla

METHOD

1. Combine flour, bran, baking powder, baking soda, fructose or sugar, and cinnamon in a large bowl. Mix well.
2. Combine whey or buttermilk, egg, and vanilla.
3. Stir liquid ingredients into dry ingredients. Add raisins.
4. Pour mixture into loaf pan coated with nonstick vegetable cooking spray and bake at 350° for 45–50 minutes. Place bread on a wire rack to cool.

Starch/Bread Exchange	1
Calories	81
Carbohydrate	15 grams
Protein	3 grams
Fat	1 gram (11%)
Saturated fat	trace
Cholesterol	12 milligrams
Fiber	3 grams
Sodium	106 milligrams

MULTIGRAIN SODA BREAD

24 Servings/Serving size: 1 slice or 1 biscuit

A quick and easy-to-make bread. It is particularly good for brunch or with bean dishes. Time and energy saver: Flatten dough to 1 inch thick and cut into squares with a knife. Bake on cookie sheet for 20 minutes.

INGREDIENTS

1	cup flour
1	cup whole-wheat flour
1	cup rye flour
1	cup rolled oats
2	Tbsp. sugar
1	Tbsp. baking powder
1	tsp. baking soda
1/4–1/2	tsp. salt (optional)
3	Tbsp. margarine
3/4	cup raisins (optional)
1 3/4	cups buttermilk

METHOD

1. Combine dry ingredients.
2. Cut in margarine.
3. Add raisins. Stir in buttermilk to make a soft dough.
4. Turn out onto a floured surface and knead about 10 times or until smooth.
5. Place on a baking sheet coated with nonstick vegetable cooking spray. Flatten dough into a circle about 2 1/2 inches thick. Cut a large X about 1/4 inch deep in top. Bake at 350° for 1 hour or until done.

With raisins:

Starch/Bread Exchange	1
Calories	102
Carbohydrate	18 grams
Protein	3 grams
Fat	2 grams (18%)
Saturated fat	trace
Cholesterol	1 milligram
Fiber	1 gram
Sodium	150 milligrams
Without added salt	138 milligrams

Without raisins:

Starch/Bread Exchange	1
Calories	86
Carbohydrate	14 grams
Protein	3 grams
Fat	2 grams(15%)
Saturated fat	trace
Cholesterol	1 milligram
Fiber	1 gram
Sodium	150 milligrams
Without added salt	138 milligrams

SCOTCH OAT SCONES

16 Servings/Serving size: 1 scone

Puffy textured triangles—the British counterparts of biscuits—are easier than biscuits to mix and cut. Oat scones are traditionally served for afternoon tea, but are also nice for breakfast, brunch, and between-meal snacks. Serve hot if possible, but taste testers liked these warm and at room temperature as well.

INGREDIENTS

1 1/2 cups flour
1   cup rolled oats
1/2   tsp. baking soda
1   tsp. cream of tartar
1   Tbsp. sugar
2   Tbsp. softened margarine
2   Tbsp. softened reduced-
       calorie margarine
1/2   cup 1% lowfat milk
1   egg white, lightly beaten
1/4   cup egg substitute

METHOD

1. In a large bowl, combine the flour, oats, salt, baking soda, cream of tartar, and sugar.
2. Using a pastry cutter or fork, cut in the margarines until the mixture resembles cornmeal.
3. Make a well in the center and add the milk and eggs. Quickly mix with a fork. Divide the dough in half. Turn out on a floured board.
4. Dip your fingers in flour and lightly flatten each dough half into a 1/2-inch thick circle. With a knife, cut each circle in half. Cut each half in half again and repeat, to make 8 triangles from each circle.
5. Place triangles on a baking sheet. Bake at 400° for 15 minutes or until golden and puffy.

Starch/Bread Exchange 1	Fat ....3 grams (30%)
Fat Exchange 1/2	Saturated fat ....1 gram
Calories 91	Cholesterol ....1 milligram
Carbohydrate ....13 grams	Fiber...trace
Protein ....3 grams	Sodium...............................73 milligrams

NO-KNEAD OATMEAL YEAST BREAD

20 Servings/Serving size: 1 slice

INGREDIENTS

1 1/4 cups water	1/4 cup warm water
3/4 cup rolled oats	1 egg white or 1/2 Tbsp. dried
1/4 cup reduced-calorie margarine	egg white plus 1 1/2 Tbsp.
1/4 cup molasses or honey	water
1 tsp. salt (optional)	2 3/4–3 cups unsifted flour
1 pkg. active dry yeast	2 Tbsp. cornflake crumbs

METHOD

1. Pour 1/3 cup water into 2-qt. glass bowl. Microwave on HIGH, 3 1/2–4 minutes or until boiling. Stir in oats, margarine, molasses, and salt. Cool to lukewarm.
2. Combine yeast with 1/4 cup warm water. Let stand a few minutes to soften yeast.
3. Add 1 cup flour and egg white to warm oatmeal mixture; beat well. Stir in softened yeast. Gradually stir in remaining flour to form a stiff batter. Cover loosely with plastic wrap.
4. Microwave on WARM (10% power) 4–6 minutes or until mixture feels warm but not hot, rotating the dish once. Let stand 15–20 minutes.
5. Microwave on WARM (10% power) 3–5 minutes or until mixture feels warm but not hot, rotating the dish once. Let stand 15–20 minutes or until dough is doubled in size.
6. Stir down batter. Coat a 2-qt. glass casserole with nonstick vegetable cooking spray. Sprinkle with cornflake crumbs, coating the bottom and sides of dish. Turn batter into casserole; sprinkle surface with crumbs.
7. Microwave on WARM (10% power), uncovered, 6–8 minutes or until mixture feels warm but not hot, rotating dish once. Let stand 15–20 minutes or until doubled (at top of dish).
8. Cover with paper towel. Microwave on MEDIUM (50% power) 10–11 minutes or until surface springs back when touched lightly, rotating dish once. Cool 5 minutes; turn out of dish. Cool completely.
9. Cut loaf into 20 slices.

Starch/Bread Exchange 1	Saturated fat .... trace
Calories 98	Cholesterol .... 0 milligrams
Carbohydrate .... 17 grams	Fiber .... 0.5 gram
Protein .... 3 grams	Sodium .... 57 milligrams
Fat .... 2 grams (18%)	Without added salt .... 28 milligrams

ROLLED OATS YEAST BREAD (NO KNEADING)

24 slices/Serving size: 1 slice

This was my teenagers' favorite bread, and they've passed the taste for it on to their children. The ends are the favorite pieces in our house, and we have been known to cut off all four "heels" even before the loaves cooled off!

INGREDIENTS

2 1/2 cups 1% lowfat milk, heated
1   cup rolled oats
1/3   cup molasses
1   Tbsp. reduced-calorie
       margarine or canola oil
1   Tbsp. dry yeast
1/2   tsp. salt (optional)
4 1/2 cups flour

METHOD

1. Pour milk over oats. Add molasses. Let set until lukewarm.
2. Add oil, yeast, salt, and 2 cups of flour and beat until dough is smooth and elastic—about 5 minutes. I use the electric mixer.
3. Add the rest of the flour, 1/2 cup at a time, stirring with a strong wooden spoon.
4. Allow to rise until double in bulk. Stir down and pour into 2 bread pans coated with nonstick vegetable cooking spray.
5. Let rise until double in bulk. Bake at 350° for 35 minutes or until done.

Starch/Bread Exchange 1 1/2	Saturated fat ....trace
Calories 117	Cholesterol ....1 milligram
Carbohydrate ....23 grams	Fiber ....1 gram
Protein ....4 grams	Sodium.............................67 milligrams
Fat..1 gram (8%)	Without added salt............19 milligrams

4 Servings/Serving size: 2 sections with 6 Tbsp. sauce

No eggs or butter in this recipe, but the cholesterol will never be missed in these filling waffles. They do take just a little longer to cook, though. This recipe makes 2 cups of batter, just the right amount for 2 waffles with 4 sections each.

INGREDIENTS

1	cup biscuit mix	**Blueberry Sauce:**	
2	Tbsp. powdered buttermilk	2	cups blueberries
3/4	cup cold water	3/4	cup water
1/4	cup crumbled tofu	12	packets artificial sweetener
1	Tbsp. vegetable oil	1	Tbsp. cornstarch
		2	tsp. lemon juice

METHOD

Sauce:
1. In saucepan, combine all ingredients unless you are using aspartame, which is added later. Bring ingredients to a boil over medium heat, stirring until sauce is clear. Remove from heat and cool a little.
2. Stir in aspartame if you are using it. Serve warm.

Waffles:
1. Spray waffle baker with nonstick vegetable cooking spray. Preheat.
2. Combine all ingredients and blend well. Use a blender for rich, smooth batter. Pour batter onto heated waffle baker and bake until crisp. Serve with blueberry sauce or any of the fruit sauces in the DESSERT section of this book.

Waffles and Sauce:

Starch/Bread Exchange 1 1/2
Medium-Fat Meat Exchange 1
Fat Exchange 1
Fruit Exchange 1
Calories 285
Carbohydrate .... 44 grams
Protein .... 7 grams
Fat .... 9 grams (28%)
Saturated fat .... trace
Cholesterol .... 0 milligrams
Fiber .... 7 grams
Sodium .... 380 milligrams

Waffles only:

Calories 193
Carbohydrate .... 22 grams
Protein .... 6 grams
Fat .... 9 grams (44%)
Saturated fat .... 1 gram
Cholesterol .... 1 milligram
Fiber .... 4 grams
Sodium .... 374 milligrams

GRANARY BREAD

32 Servings/Serving size: 1 slice

An old favorite that always makes the house smell so homey. Requires 2–24 hours in the refrigerator, so it is a good selection when you don't have a large block of time. You can mix and shape it one night and bake it the next.

INGREDIENTS

3 1/2–4 1/2 cups flour
2 1/2 cups graham flour
2   pkg. active dry yeast
1   tsp. salt
1/3 cup honey
3   Tbsp. reduced-calorie
       margarine
2 1/2 cups hot tap water
       Cooking oil or spray

METHOD

1. Combine 2 cups flour, yeast, and salt in a large bowl. Stir well. Add honey, margarine, and hot water. Beat with electric mixer at medium speed for 2 minutes. Scrape bowl. Beat in 1 cup more flour and 1/2 cup graham flour. Beat at high speed for 1 minute or until thick and elastic.
2. Stir in remaining graham flour with wooden spoon. Gradually stir in enough of remaining flour to make soft dough that leaves sides of bowl. Knead on floured board 5–10 minutes until smooth and elastic.
3. Cover and let rest for 20 minutes. Punch down. Divide dough in half. Shape into 2 round loaves about 8 inches in diameter.
4. Place in 8-inch loaf pans coated with nonstick vegetable cooking spray. Brush with oil or coat with vegetable spray. Cover with plastic wrap. Refrigerate for 2–24 hours.
5. When ready to bake, remove from refrigerator, uncover, and let stand 10 minutes. Make 6 1/4-inch deep cuts, spoke fashion, in tops of loaves. Bake at 400° for 30–40 minutes. Use lower oven rack.
6. Remove from pans. Cool on wire racks.

Starch/Bread Exchange	1	Saturated fat	trace
Calories	101	Cholesterol	0 milligrams
Carbohydrate	20 grams	Fiber	1 gram
Protein	3 grams	Sodium	84 milligrams
Fat	9 grams (44%)		

BOSTON BROWN BREAD

20 Servings/Serving size: 1 slice

Homemade brown bread bakes about as fast as opening and heating a can of ready-made. Baked beans are not the only companion for brown bread—try it with casseroles and stews.

INGREDIENTS

1/2	cup graham or whole-wheat flour
1/4	cup flour
1/4	cup cornmeal
1/2	tsp. baking powder
1/4	tsp. baking soda
1/4	tsp. salt (optional)
1/4	cup egg substitute
2	Tbsp. molasses
2	Tbsp. corn oil
1/2	cup buttermilk or sour milk
1/4	cup raisins

METHOD

1. Lightly spray 3 8-oz. glass custard cups with nonstick vegetable cooking spray.
2. Sift together the flours, cornmeal, baking powder, soda, and salt.
3. In mixing bowl, combine the egg, molasses, and oil.
4. Add the flour mixture to molasses mixture alternately with milk; mix well. Stir in raisins.
5. Spoon into measuring cups. Microwave 2 minutes on HIGH. Rearrange cups. Microwave 2–2 1/2 minutes on HIGH or until done. Tops may be moist. Cool in cups 5 minutes.
6. Serve warm, sliced.

Starch/Bread Exchange	1/2	Saturated fat	trace
Calories	50	Cholesterol	0 milligrams
Carbohydrate	7 grams	Fiber	1 gram
Protein	1 gram	Sodium	67 milligrams
Fat	2 grams (30%)	Without added salt	38 milligrams

HOMEMADE SESAME CRACKERS

50 2 x 2-inch Crackers/Serving size: 3 crackers

Something nutritious for the cracker barrel.

INGREDIENTS

1	cup whole-wheat flour
1	cup flour
1/2	tsp. salt
1 1/2	tsp. baking powder
1/4	cup yogurt
2	Tbsp. sesame seeds
1	Tbsp. corn oil
3/4	cup ice water

METHOD

1. Spray cookie sheet with nonstick vegetable cooking spray.
2. Sift together the first four ingredients. Cut in the yogurt.
3. Toast the sesame seeds in the oil and add to batter.
4. Mix in ice water. Knead lightly (20 strokes).
5. Roll to 1/8 inch thick. Cut with knife or cookie cutter.
6. Prick all over with a fork. Bake on cookie sheet at 350° for 10 minutes or until crackers are light brown. Cool on a wire rack. They will crisp as they cool.
7. Store in a tightly covered container.

Starch/Bread Exchange	1	Saturated fat	trace
Calories	70	Cholesterol	trace
Carbohydrate	11 grams	Fiber	1 gram
Protein	2 grams	Sodium	109 milligrams
Fat	2 grams (26%)	Without added salt	41 milligrams

ROLLED OATS CRACKERS

90 Crackers/Serving size: 3 crackers

Keep these on hand for snacking plain or with cheese and fruit. They travel well. I took a boxful on a 1,000-mile trip in our camper.

INGREDIENTS

3   cups uncooked rolled oats
2   cups unbleached flour
1   cup wheat germ
2   Tbsp. sugar
1/4   cup corn oil
1 1/4 cups water

METHOD

1. Combine ingredients and press into 2 large cookie sheets that have been coated with nonstick vegetable cooking spray. Press dough as thin as you can, pushing from the center to make the dough around the edges as thick as in the center.
2. Mark into squares or diamonds. Sprinkle very lightly with salt if you wish, but we like them plain.
3. Bake in 350° oven for 20–25 minutes or until crisp and lightly browned. Cool and store in airtight container.

Starch/Bread Exchange	1	
Fat Exchange	1	
Calories	128	
Carbohydrate	18 grams	
Protein	5 grams	
Fat	4 grams (28%)	
Saturated fat	trace	
Cholesterol	0 milligrams	
Fiber	2 grams	
Sodium	1 milligram	

APPLE-CHEESE PANCAKES*

4 Servings/Serving size: 2 small pancakes

Serve these pancakes for breakfast, brunch, or lunch. They could even be a dessert after a light meal.

INGREDIENTS

1	cup low-fat cottage or part-skim ricotta cheese
1 1/4	cup apple, grated
1/2	cup flour
1/4	cup whole-wheat flour
1	Tbsp. honey
1	Tbsp. lemon juice
1	Tbsp. sunflower seeds or chopped almonds
1/2	tsp. cinnamon
	Dash of nutmeg or allspice
1/2	tsp. salt (optional)
1/4	cup egg substitute
4	egg whites

METHOD

1. Mix all ingredients together except egg whites.
2. Beat egg whites until stiff and fold into batter.
3. Cook pancakes in nonstick skillet or skillet sprayed with nonstick vegetable cooking spray until brown on both sides and cooked inside. They take longer than plain flour pancakes.
4. Serve with fruit sauce (page 174), maple syrup, or preserves over cottage cheese or yogurt.

*Not recommended for low-sodium diets if salt is added.

Fruit Exchange	1	Fat	7 grams (29%)
High-Fat Meat Exchange	1	Saturated fat	3 grams
Starch/Bread Exchange	1	Cholesterol	19 milligrams
Calories	219	Fiber	2 grams
Carbohydrate	30 grams	Sodium	461 milligrams
Protein	9 grams	Without added salt	174 milligrams

8 Servings/Serving size: 1 cup

Let your food processor help to make cholesterol-free egg noodles. Makes about 1 pound of uncooked pasta or 2 pounds cooked.

INGREDIENTS

2 1/2 cups flour
1/2   cup egg substitute
1/2   tsp. salt (optional)
1/3   cup water
1   tsp. olive oil

METHOD

1. In a food processor bowl with steel blade, process flour, egg substitute, and salt until mixture resembles cornmeal. With processor running, slowly pour water and oil through the feed tube. Process until the dough forms a ball (about 15 seconds). Remove and cover dough; let rest 10 minutes.
2. Divide dough into fourths. Roll each piece into a 12-inch square, 1/16 inch thick. Let stand 20 minutes to dry the surface.
3. Roll up dough loosely and cut into 1/4-inch slices. Cook a few minutes in rapidly boiling water or spread out strips to dry and then freeze to cook later.

Starch/Bread Exchange	2	Saturated fat	trace
Calories	145	Cholesterol	0 milligrams
Carbohydrate	28 grams	Fiber	1 gram
Protein	6 grams	Sodium	172 milligrams
Fat	1 gram (6%)	Without added salt	28 milligrams

EGGPLANT RICOTTA BAKE

12 Servings/Serving size: 1 cup

I call this "eggplant for people who think they don't like eggplant." This recipe can easily be halved if you want to be very cautious the first time you make it. It's just as delicious with soy mozzarella.

INGREDIENTS

3   medium eggplants with firm, smooth skin
1 1/2 cups onion, chopped
1 1/2 tsp. garlic, minced
2   cups nonfat ricotta cheese
1 1/2 cups part-skim mozzarella, grated
3/4   cup wheat germ
1   tsp. oregano
1   tsp. basil
2–3   large tomatoes, sliced

METHOD

1. Spray cookie sheet with nonstick vegetable spray. Slice the eggplant into 1/3-inch circles. Place on cookie sheet. Put a few grains of salt on each slice.
2. Bake for 15 minutes at 350°. Saute onions and garlic until soft. Combine with the cheeses.
3. Combine wheat germ and spices. Coat a large baking pan with vegetable spray. Layer ingredients this way: eggplant, wheat germ, cheese, tomato, eggplant, tomato, wheat germ. Cover pan. Bake at 350° for 30 minutes.
4. Uncover and bake 5 minutes. Serve warm. Reheats beautifully in the microwave oven.

Lean Meat Exchange 1 1/2	Fat.....................................4 grams (24%)
Vegetable Exchange 2	Saturated fat ....2 grams
Calories 148	Cholesterol..........................8 milligrams
Carbohydrate ....14 grams	Fiber..3 grams
Protein ....14 grams	Sodium...............................81 milligrams

BAKED BEANS IN THE PRESSURE COOKER*

8 Servings/Serving size: 1/4 cup

We love baked beans, and now a grandson has developed a taste for Grammie's Baked Beans. This is the recipe whether they are cooked in the pressure cooker or on the woodstove. Best if cooked several hours before eaten, but we usually sneak a spoonful as soon as the pressure is down.

INGREDIENTS

2	cups (1 lb.) yellow eye, soldier, or pea beans
2–3	Tbsp. reduced-calorie margarine
3	Tbsp. molasses
2	Tbsp. dark brown sugar or sugar substitute
1	tsp. dry mustard
3/4	tsp. salt (optional)
1/8	tsp. pepper
	Boiling water

METHOD

1. Pick over beans, rinse, and soak overnight. Drain. Place in pressure cooker with other ingredients, using enough boiling water to just cover beans. Stir.
2. Clean rim of pressure cooker of any food or moisture. Cover pan. Cook at 15 lbs. pressure for 40 minutes. Allow pressure to go down on its own.

*For occasional use only, due to sugar content.

Starch/Bread Exchange	1	Saturated fat	trace
Calories	94	Cholesterol	0 milligrams
Carbohydrate	15 grams	Fiber	3 grams
Protein	4 grams	Sodium	268 milligrams
Fat	2 grams (19%)	Without added salt	52 milligrams

SCALLOPED CORN*

4 Servings/Serving size: 1/4 recipe

Make this when you have an assortment of leftovers and you want one dish to tie everything together. Energy-saving tip: Bake muffins and heat up some of those leftovers in the oven while it is on for the Scalloped Corn.

INGREDIENTS

1   can (15 1/2 oz.) cream-style corn
1   cup skim milk (fresh, dry, or evaporated)
1/4   cup egg substitute
       Pepper
6   saltines (with or without salted tops), crushed
2   Tbsp. additional crumbs (This is a good use for those crumbs that are left in the party cereal mix jar.)

METHOD

1. Coat a 1 1/2-qt. baking dish with nonstick vegetable cooking spray.
2. Mix corn, milk, egg substitute, pepper, and 8 crushed crackers. Top with crumbs.
3. Bake at 350° for 45 minutes.

*Not recommended for low-sodium diets unless unsalted saltines are used.

Starch/Bread Exchange 2	Saturated fat ....trace
Calories 150	Cholesterol ....3 grams
Carbohydrate ....27 grams	Fiber...3 grams
Protein ....6 grams	Sodium...........................423 milligrams
Fat....................................2 grams (12%)	with unsalted saltines...384 milligrams

6 Servings/Serving size: 1 cup

This is a good way to introduce tofu to skeptics. If you have a favorite chili recipe and want to introduce tofu to the people you cook for, try substituting tofu for 1/2 of the meat. Serve with bread and salad followed by something cool and sweet for dessert, such as the Fruit Plate with Creamy Dessert Sauce in the DESSERT section.

INGREDIENTS

1   cup onions, chopped
2   tsp. safflower oil
1   clove garlic, minced
1/2   lb. tofu, cubed
1 1/2 tsp. chili powder
1   tsp. cumin
1   can (28 oz.) low-sodium
      tomatoes with liquid
1   can (15 oz.) kidney beans

METHOD

1. Saute onions and garlic in oil.
2. Add remaining ingredients. Stir.
3. Simmer about 20 minutes.
4. Serve over rice.

*Not recommended for low-sodium diets if prepared with regular tomatoes.

Starch/Bread Exchange 1	Saturated fat..................................1 gram
Medium-Meat Exchange........................1	Cholesterol ....0 grams
Vegetable Exchange 1	Fiber...8 grams
Calories 186	Sodium...........................278 milligrams
Carbohydrate ....21 grams	with regular tomatoes ..517 milligrams
Protein......................................12 grams	
Fat....................................6 grams (29%)	

CRUSTLESS ZUCCHINI TOFU QUICHE*

6 Servings/Serving size: 1 cup

This dish was my introduction to modifying a recipe to include tofu. The original recipe had no tofu but used more cheese and also used margarine when sauteeing the vegetables. This also works well as an appetizer. Cook in oblong dish, cool, and slice into small squares. Reheats nicely on an electric warming tray, an electric skillet, or a toaster oven.

INGREDIENTS

4	cups zucchini, fresh or frozen, shredded
1	cup onions, chopped
1 1/2	cloves garlic, minced
3/4	cup egg substitute
1	Tbsp. sherry or lemon juice
3/4	tsp. basil
1/4	tsp. thyme
3/4	tsp. oregano
1/4	tsp. ginger
1	cup (4 oz.) low-fat cheddar cheese, shredded
1/4	cup Parmesan cheese
1/2	cup tofu, crumbled
	Italian bread crumbs

METHOD

1. In a deep 9-inch pie plate or shallow casserole, microwave zucchini, onions, and garlic 7 minutes on HIGH, stirring twice.
2. Beat egg substitute; add wine and seasonings. Add to vegetables.
3. Stir in cheeses and tofu. Sprinkle crumbs on top.
4. Microwave 10 minutes on HIGH or until nearly set in center.

⚖ Balance with lower-fat dishes on days you use this recipe. *Not recommended for low-sodium diets.

Lean Meat Exchange	2	Fat	6 grams (38%)
Vegetable Exchange	1	Saturated fat	2 grams
Calories	142	Cholesterol	9 grams
Carbohydrate	7 grams	Fiber	3 grams
Protein	15 grams	Sodium	419 milligrams

STUFFED ZUCCHINI

6 Servings/Serving size: 1/2 zucchini

The smoky flavor of provolone cheese adds zing to this dish.

INGREDIENTS

3	zucchini, 6–8 inches long
1	cup mushrooms, chopped
2	Tbsp. onions, finely chopped
2	Tbsp. reduced-calorie margarine
2	Tbsp. flour
1/2	tsp. salt (optional)
1/2	tsp. oregano
1	cup (4 oz.) nonfat mozzarella or provolone cheese, shredded
2	Tbsp. nonfat plain yogurt Freshly ground pepper

METHOD

1. Cut zucchini in half lengthwise. Cook in boiling water 4–5 minutes or until tender-crisp (I use an electric skillet). Remove pulp, leaving a 1/4-inch shell; chop pulp.
2. Saute mushrooms and onions in margarine. Stir in flour and seasonings. Turn off heat.
3. Stir in cheese, yogurt, pepper, and chopped zucchini. Fill shells.
4. Broil 4–5 minutes or until cheese melts. Note: Zucchini can be prepared to this step, covered, and refrigerated. Then broil 5–7 minutes.

With nonfat mozzarella:		With provolone:	
Lean Meat Exchange	1	High-Fat Meat Exchange	1
Calories	62	Calories	103
Carbohydrate	4 grams	Carbohydrate	4 grams
Protein	7 grams	Protein	6 grams
Fat	2 grams (29%)	Fat	7 grams (61%)
Saturated fat	trace	Saturated fat	4 grams
Cholesterol	3 milligrams	Cholesterol	14 milligrams
Fiber	2 grams	Fiber	2 grams
Sodium	334 milligrams	Sodium	398 milligrams
Without added salt	142 milligrams	Without added salt	206 milligrams

"CREAMED" CAULIFLOWER

4 Servings/Serving size: 1 cup

A unique way to serve low-calorie cauliflower when there is an abundance of it in your garden or in the grocery store. This is such a light main dish that I'd suggest a spicy muffin from the BREADS section, a substantial salad from SALADS, and something hearty such as Tofu Cheesecake from the DESSERT section. Try this recipe with all of your favorite vegetables. You can even add small amounts of leftovers such as cooked brown rice, grated cheese, or couscous or other cooked cereals.

INGREDIENTS

1 1/2 lb. fresh (or two 10-oz. pkg.
     of frozen) cauliflower
1/4   tsp. butter-flavored granules
1/2   tsp. parsley flakes or 1 Tbsp.
     fresh parsley, chopped
1   cup (8 oz.) 1% low-fat cottage
     cheese

METHOD

1. Cook, drain, and mash cauliflower. Combine with rest of ingredients.
2. Spoon into baking dish coated with nonstick vegetable cooking spray. Bake at 350° for 30 minutes.

Vegetable Exchange	1	Fat	1 gram (11%)
Lean Meat Exchange	1	Saturated fat	trace
Calories	85	Cholesterol	3 grams
Carbohydrate	9 grams	Fiber	4 grams
Protein	10 grams	Sodium	219 milligrams

BEAN CASSEROLE*

6 Servings/Serving size: 1 cup

The electric skillet is one of my favorite appliances (when the woodstove isn't going). This casserole is a natural for the skillet. We like this with the Multi-Grain Soda Bread in the BREAD section.

INGREDIENTS

1	Tbsp. vegetable oil
1	clove garlic, minced
2	medium onions, sliced
1	can (14 oz.) low-sodium whole tomatoes or equivalent fresh or frozen
1	can (19 oz.) red kidney beans, drained
1	can (16 oz.) chick peas (garbanzo beans)
1/2	tsp. dried oregano
10	oz. fresh spinach, washed
1/4	tsp. freshly ground pepper

METHOD

1. Heat oil over medium heat; cook garlic and onions, stirring occasionally, for 3 minutes or until softened. Add tomatoes, breaking up with spoon.
2. Add kidney beans, chick peas, and oregano; bring to simmer.
3. Add spinach, cover, and simmer until spinach is wilted, about 2 minutes. Season with pepper to taste.
4. For a change of pace, add some cooked turkey with the onion and add chili powder.

*Not recommended for low-sodium diets.

Starch/Bread Exchange	2	Fat	4 grams (15%)
Vegetable Exchange	1	Saturated fat	1 gram
Meat Exchange	1	Cholesterol	0 milligrams
Calories	236	Fiber	14 grams
Carbohydrate	39 grams	Sodium	572 milligrams
Protein	11 grams		

BETTY'S MACARONI AND CHEESE*

4 Servings/Serving size: 1/2 cup

This recipe was developed before the need for less sodium and fat was recognized. It is so good that I am giving you the original directions below but suggesting the following changes here for today's lifestyle: Mix the flour with a little of the milk to make a smooth paste. Add the rest of the milk and only 1–2 Tbsp. of margarine. Microwave 4–5 minutes, stirring once or twice. Add 4 oz. of cheddar cheese and 4 oz. of some type of low-fat, low-sodium cheese, and use salt-free seasoning. Energy-saving tip: To cook macaroni, boil water and add macaroni as usual. Stir until it comes to a rolling boil. Cover and remove from heat. Let stand for the cooking time indicated on the package. Drain.

INGREDIENTS

1	cup uncooked macaroni (2 cups cooked)
3	Tbsp. reduced-calorie margarine
3	Tbsp. flour
1 1/2	cups 1% milk
8	oz. sharp low-fat cheddar cheese, cubed
1/2	tsp. seasoned salt (optional)
1/4	tsp. celery salt (optional)

METHOD

1. In medium casserole microwave margarine 40–45 seconds on HIGH.
2. Add flour and stir until smooth. Stir in milk; microwave on HIGH, stirring once.
3. Add cheese and seasonings and microwave 1 minute on HIGH. Combine macaroni and cheese sauce. Microwave 2 minutes on HIGH or until heated through. Cover. Let stand 10 minutes.

*Not recommended for low-sodium diets.

Starch/Bread Exchange	2	Saturated fat	4 grams
Lean Meat Exchange	2	Cholesterol	24 milligrams
Calories	298	Fiber	1 gram
Carbohydrate	31 grams	Sodium	1376 milligrams
Protein	21 grams	Without added salt	1018 milligrams
Fat	10 grams (30%)		

INGREDIENTS

2	pkg. (10 oz. each) frozen chopped spinach
1	qt. spaghetti sauce with mushrooms
1/2	cup dry red wine
1/4	tsp. garlic powder
	Dash of nutmeg
2	cups (16 oz.) low-fat cottage cheese

1/4	cup Parmesan cheese
1/4	cup egg substitute
	Dash of pepper
6	uncooked lasagna noodles
8	oz. fat-free mozzarella cheese, sliced
1	can (3 1/4 oz.) pitted ripe olives, drained and sliced

METHOD

1. Microwave both packages of spinach 7–8 minutes on HIGH. Drain and squeeze out moisture, save juice for soup. Set aside.
2. Combine spaghetti sauce, wine, garlic powder, and nutmeg in 2-qt. bowl. Microwave 5–6 minutes on HIGH or until hot. Remove 1 1/2 cups sauce and set aside. Add spinach to remainder of sauce in bowl.
3. Mix cottage cheese, Parmesan cheese, egg substitute, and pepper. Pour 1/2 spinach sauce into bottom of a 2-qt. (8 x 12-inch) oblong dish.
4. Place 3 uncooked noodles over the sauce, then add 1/2 cottage cheese mixture and 1/2 mozzarella. Repeat layers.
5. Stir olives into reserved sauce and pour over top of casserole.
6. Microwave 5 minutes on HIGH, then 20 minutes on MEDIUM-HIGH (70% power). Let stand 10 minutes before serving.

*Not recommended for low-sodium diets.

Starch/Bread Exchange 2	Fat ....11 grams (27%)
Medium-Fat Meat Exchange 2	Saturated fat ....2 grams
Vegetable Exchange 2	Cholesterol........................10 milligrams
Calories 367	Fiber..7 grams
Carbohydrate ....42 grams	Sodium..........................1039 milligrams
Protein.....................................25 grams	

TURKEY-ASPARAGUS BRUNCH BAKE*

10 Servings/Serving size: approximately 3 x 4-inch square

This was one of my favorite taste tests. I love asparagus and wanted a recipe to serve a crowd without last-minute preparations. Broccoli may be substituted for asparagus.

INGREDIENTS

1 1/2 lb.	fresh asparagus cut into 1 1/2-inch pieces or 2 pkg. (10 oz.) frozen asparagus, divided	1	cup flour
1	lb. raw turkey, ground	1/4	cup grated Parmesan cheese
1	medium onion, chopped	1	tsp. lemon pepper
1/2	cup sweet red pepper, chopped	1/2	tsp. salt (optional)
2	cups egg substitute	1	tsp. dried tarragon, crushed
2	cups skim milk	1	cup (4 oz.) lowfat Swiss cheese, shredded
		4	sweet red pepper rings

METHOD

1. Cook asparagus until tender-crisp. Do not overcook!
2. Saute turkey, onions, and red pepper until no pink remains in the turkey.
3. Spray 13 x 9 x 2-inch baking pan with nonstick vegetable cooking spray. Spread meat mixture in baking pan. Cover with asparagus. Reserve a few perfect tips for garnish.
4. Combine eggs, milk, flour, Parmesan cheese, lemon pepper, salt, and tarragon in blender or mixing bowl. Blend until smooth.
5. Pour egg mixture over all in baking dish. Bake at 375° for 30 minutes or until knife inserted near center comes out clean.
6. Sprinkle with Swiss cheese. Put back in oven with heat turned off for 3–5 minutes until cheese melts. Decorate with reserved asparagus and red pepper slices.

*Not recommended for low-sodium diets if salt is added.

Starch/Bread Exchange	1	Saturated fat	3 grams
Medium-Fat Meat Exchange	3	Cholesterol	2 grams
Calories	232	Fiber	2 grams
Carbohydrate	18 grams	Sodium	457 milligrams
Protein	22 grams	Without added salt	342 milligrams
Fat	8 grams (31%)		

BAKED CHICKEN NUGGETS

4 Servings/Serving size: 1/4 recipe with 2 Tbsp. sauce

I used thigh meat for these nuggets because chicken legs were 49 cents a pound the day I shopped. For about $3 I got enough drumsticks for a batch of Microwave Chicken with Barbecue Mustard (this section) plus the meat for these nuggets plus trimmings and skin for a batch of Chicken Stock (see Soup section). Chicken breast contains less fat, thus fewer calories than chicken thighs, so if you are eliminating as much fat as possible from your diet, watch for specials on chicken breast. You may never want to eat the high-fat version again!

INGREDIENTS

2	egg whites, fresh or reconstituted dried	1	tsp. onion flakes
1	Tbsp. water	1	lb. skinless, boneless chicken, cut into 2-inch squares
1	cup plain dry bread crumbs		**Dipping Sauce**
1	tsp. dry mustard	1/2	cup plain low-fat yogurt
1	tsp. paprika	1	Tbsp. honey
1	tsp. tarragon or basil	1	Tbsp. Dijon mustard
1/2	tsp. black pepper		

METHOD

1. Stir ingredients together.
2. Spray large baking sheet with nonstick vegetable cooking spray or use nonstick pan.
3. Combine egg whites and water.
4. Combine crumbs, mustard, paprika, tarragon, pepper, and onion in plastic bowl with secure cover.
5. Coat each piece of chicken with egg white and then place in crumb bowl. Do a few at a time, place cover on bowl and shake to coat with crumbs.
6. Place nuggets on baking sheet. Bake at 375° for 25 minutes.

Nuggets with sauce:
Starch/Bread Exchange....................1 1/2
Lean Meat Exchange.............................3
Calories 216
Carbohydrate ....21 grams
Protein ....24 grams
Fat ....4 grams (17%)
Saturated fat.................................1 gram
Cholesterol...................... 69 milligrams
Fiber ....1 gram

Sodium.............................369 milligrams
Sauce:
Calories 25
Carbohydrate ....3 grams
Protein ....2 grams
Fat ....0.5 grams (18%)
Saturated fat ....trace
Cholesterol..........................2 milligrams
Fiber...trace
Sodium...............................67 milligrams

CHICKEN PIQUANT

8 Servings/Serving size: 2 oz.

Elegant but easy recipe from a woman who is adept in the kitchen as well as in the board room. I froze this in a square plastic container and took it on a camping trip. We grilled the chicken one evening and had the leftovers in a chef salad for lunch the next day. All tasters agreed it was delicious. Energy-saving tip: Plan to have leftovers. It is called planning ahead.

INGREDIENTS

4	whole boneless, skinless chicken breasts, split, or 8 chicken leg sections
1 1/2	cups rose or dry wine
1/2	cup reduced-calorie soy sauce
2	Tbsp. corn oil
4	Tbsp. water
2	cloves garlic, sliced
2	tsp. ground ginger
1/2	tsp. oregano
2	Tbsp. brown sugar

METHOD

1. Arrange chicken in baking dish.
2. Combine rest of ingredients to make marinade. Pour marinade over chicken.
3. Refrigerate overnight or freeze. Return to room temperature.
4. Bake covered at 375° for 1 hour. Or to grill, remove from marinade and brush marinade on chicken as it cooks.

Vegetable Exchange	1	Fat	5 gram (32%)
Lean Meat Exchange	2	Saturated fat	trace
Calories	141	Cholesterol	63 milligrams
Carbohydrate	6 grams	Fiber	0 milligrams
Protein	18 grams	Sodium	149 milligrams

CHICKEN WITH MUSTARD BARBECUE SAUCE

6 Servings/Serving size: 3 oz.

Use any combination of drumsticks, thighs, or wings as an appetizer or for dinner. Leftover sauce is delicious spread on turkey sausage and grilled outdoors. Energy-saving tip: The microwave oven is ideal for hot weather cooking. It releases much less heat into the kitchen than conventional cooking.

INGREDIENTS

1 3/4 lb. skinned drumsticks
    (approximately)
1/3 cup spicy brown mustard
3   Tbsp. dark corn syrup
2   cloves garlic, minced
1/4 tsp. hot pepper sauce

METHOD

1. Arrange chicken spoke-fashion in a round dish, thick ends toward the outside of the dish.
2. Combine rest of ingredients. Spoon over chicken to coat well. Cover with plastic wrap. Microwave on HIGH for 12 minutes. Remove from oven.
3. Stir juices in chicken dish into remaining sauce. Cover and microwave on IIIGII for 5 minutes. Pass separately as a dipping sauce.

Fruit Exchange	1	Fat	5 grams (25%)
Lean Meat Exchange	3	Saturated fat	1 gram
Calories	177	Cholesterol	87 milligrams
Carbohydrate	9 grams	Fiber	trace
Protein	24 grams	Sodium	281 milligrams

TURKEY MEATBALLS

4 Servings/Serving size: 3 oz.

If you haven't tried using ground turkey instead of beef, this recipe could be a tasty introduction. These meatballs would be welcome at a potluck supper. Ideal for a small electric casserole. Serve as a baked potato topping or over rice or noodles. Energy-saving tip: Make a double batch and bake them in the oven along with potatoes or rice.

INGREDIENTS

1	lb. raw turkey, ground
1	small onion, minced
1/4	cup bread crumbs (For more fiber, use rolled oats.)
1 1/2	Tbsp. water
1/4	cup egg substitute
1	pkg. brown gravy mix

METHOD

1. Combine all ingredients except gravy mix. Shape into meatballs and brown in nonstick skillet. (An omelet pan works fine.)
2. Mix gravy mix according to package directions. Add meatballs and simmer for 1 hour.

⚖️Balance with lower-fat dishes on days you use this recipe.

Starch/Bread Exchange	1/2	Fat	12 grams (47%)
Medium-Fat Meat Exchange	3	Saturated fat	3 grams
Calories	232	Cholesterol	72 milligrams
Carbohydrate	9 grams	Fiber	1 gram
Protein	22 grams	Sodium	378 milligrams

6 Servings/Serving size: 1/6 recipe

This is fast and easy any way you cook it, but I prefer the electric skillet. Put the rice in the microwave just before you start this, and everything will be ready at the same time. Rice does not cook faster in the microwave, but it is easier because it requires no tending. Use a large flat-bottomed casserole for the rice so it will not boil over. Consult your microwave book for directions. Energy-saving tip: Have everything ready before you start cooking or some foods may overcook if they have to wait for the next step. Or let family members or friends help with the chopping and stirring.

INGREDIENTS

1	lb. ground raw turkey
1	lb. onions, chopped
1	small bunch celery, sliced
	Salt and pepper to taste
2	cups homemade chicken broth
1	Tbsp. molasses
1	lb. mung bean sprouts
2	Tbsp. cornstarch
4	Tbsp. lite soy sauce

METHOD

1. Saute turkey, onions, and celery.
2. When turkey is no longer pink, add salt, pepper, and broth and cook for about 10 minutes.
3. Add molasses and sprouts. Cook 10 minutes longer.
4. Mix cornstarch and soy sauce. Add to pan. Stir until thickened. If more sauce is needed, add more broth or water.
5. Serve over hot, cooked rice and pass around the soy sauce.

⚖ Balance with lower-fat dishes on days you use this recipe.

Starch/Bread Exchange	1	Fat	7 grams (34%)
Meat Exchange	2	Saturated fat	2 grams
Calories	183	Cholesterol	61 milligrams
Carbohydrate	14 grams	Fiber	3 grams
Protein	16 grams	Sodium	160 milligrams

CRISPY BAKED CHICKEN

2 Servings/Serving size: 2 oz.

Cornflake crumbs give this skinless chicken a crisp coating even in the microwave oven. Energy-saving tip: The most energy-efficient way to cook small amounts of meat is in the microwave.

INGREDIENTS

1   chicken breast, split and
       skinned
1/4   cup skim milk
1/4   cup cornflake crumbs
1/4   tsp. rosemary or coriander
       Freshly ground pepper

METHOD

1. Rinse and dry chicken pieces thoroughly. Dip in milk.
2. Mix cornflake crumbs with rosemary or coriander and pepper. Roll chicken in the seasoned crumbs.
3. Place on microwave-safe roasting rack. Cover with paper towel.
4. Microwave 4–6 minutes on HIGH or until done.

Lean Meat Exchange............................2	Saturated fat.......................................trace
Calories...106	Cholesterol.........................60 milligrams
Carbohydrate.............................4 grams	Fiber...0 grams
Protein.......................................18 grams	Sodium.............................119 milligrams
Fat...................................2 grams (20%)	

CHICKEN AND FRUIT SALAD

4 Servings/Serving size: 1/4 recipe

Here's a use for that chicken you cooked when making chicken stock (see SOUPS). The carrot that cooked with the chicken stock is good in the salad, too.

INGREDIENTS

2–3	cups cooked chicken, cubed
1	large peach or nectarine, sliced
1/2–1	cup strawberries or raspberries, sliced
2	Tbsp. walnuts, broken
1/2	cup low-fat plain yogurt
1	Tbsp. honey
1/4	tsp. fresh ginger, grated
1	fresh cantaloupe, sliced
	Crisp lettuce leaves

METHOD

1. Combine chicken, peach, strawberries, and walnuts.
2. Stir together yogurt, honey, and ginger.
3. On individual salad plates or on a platter, arrange lettuce leaves and cantaloupe slices.
4. Top with chicken mixture.
5. Pour yogurt dressing on salad.

Lean Meat Exchange	3	Fat	8 grams (27%)
Fruit Exchange	2	Saturated fat	2 grams
Calories	268	Cholesterol	66 milligrams
Carbohydrate	24 grams	Fiber	6 grams
Protein	25 grams	Sodium	86 milligrams

OVEN-CRISP SESAME DRUMSTICKS

6 Servings/Serving size: 1 chicken leg

Energy-saving tip: Make this a part of an oven meal. Or make a double batch and have cold chicken ready for the next day.

INGREDIENTS

1/4	cup egg substitute
1	Tbsp. corn oil
1/4	cup water
1/2	cup sesame seeds
2/3	cup whole-wheat flour
	Pinch of salt
1	tsp. paprika
6	chicken legs, skinned and separated at the joint (about 1 1/2 lb.)

METHOD

1. In a small bowl, beat together the egg, oil, and water.
2. In a dish, mix together sesame seed, flour, salt, and paprika.
3. Dip drumsticks into egg mixture, then into flour mixture and place on a baking sheet coated with nonstick vegetable cooking spray.
4. Bake at 400° for 25–30 minutes. Serve hot or cold.

⚖ Balance with lower-fat dishes on days you use this recipe.

Meat Exchange.........................3	Fat..................12 grams (44%)
Starch/Bread Exchange..........1	Saturated fat..............2 grams
Fat Exchange 1	Cholesterol........87 milligrams
Calories 248	Fiber ....1 gram
Carbohydrate ....11 grams	Sodium.............116 milligrams
Protein ....24 grams	

OVEN-"FRIED" CHICKEN

8 Servings/Serving size: 1/2 breast

Energy-saving tip: Make baked potatoes at the same time.

INGREDIENTS

1/3	cup low-fat plain yogurt
2	Tbsp. lemon juice
1	Tbsp. peeled, minced ginger-root
1	clove garlic, minced
1/2	tsp. ground cumin
1/8	tsp. ground red pepper
4	whole chicken breasts, halved and skinned (32 oz.)
1 1/4 cups oat-bran cereal flakes, crushed	

METHOD

1. Combine yogurt, lemon juice, gingerroot, garlic, cumin, and pepper.
2. Add chicken, turning to thoroughly coat chicken.
3. Cover and refrigerate at least 2 hours, turning occasionally.
4. Spray 13 x 9-inch baking dish with nonstick vegetable cooking spray.
5. Remove chicken from sauce with as much sauce as possible. Coat with cereal.
6. Place fleshy side up in pan in a single layer.
7. Bake at 400° about 50 minutes or until brown and tender.

Lean Meat Exchange	3	Fat	3 grams (13%)
Starch/Bread Exchange	1	Saturated fat	1 gram
Vegetable Exchange	1	Cholesterol	69 milligrams
Calories	203	Fiber	5 grams
Carbohydrate	22 grams	Sodium	86 milligrams
Protein	22 grams		

CHICKEN BAKED IN SPICY YOGURT

8 Servings/Serving size: 1/8 of recipe

I used 3 1/2 lbs. skinned drumsticks and served the finished product at a picnic-on-the-porch. Rated superb finger food. Energy-saving tip: Plan to make this as part of an oven-cooked meal.

INGREDIENTS

3 1/2 lb. broiler-fryer chicken, cut
      into serving pieces, or 3 lbs.
      chicken legs or breasts
1   cup low-fat plain yogurt
1/2 tsp. ground cumin
1/2 tsp. dry mustard
1/4 tsp. red pepper flakes
1/4 tsp. ground ginger
1   clove garlic, minced
1/2 cup scallions, sliced
      diagonally into 1-inch pieces,
      including green tops

METHOD

1. Rinse chicken under cold, running water; dry with paper towels.
2. Stir together all the other ingredients, except scallions.
3. Add chicken and turn pieces to coat with yogurt mixture. Cover and refrigerate 8 hours or longer.
4. Spray 13 x 9-inch pan with nonstick vegetable cooking spray.
5. Arrange chicken in pan. Cover with remaining sauce.
6. Bake uncovered at 350° for about 1 hour.
7. Garnish with scallions.

Lean Meat Exchange..............................4
Calories 177
Carbohydrate ....2 grams
Protein ....31 grams
Fat....................................5 grams (25%)

Saturated fat.................................1 gram
Cholesterol......................122 milligrams
Fiber...0 grams
Sodium..........................149 milligrams

CHICKEN & BROCCOLI WITH MUSHROOM SAUCE

4 Servings/Serving size: 4 oz.

This recipe calls for both chicken broth and cooked chicken. See directions in SOUP section. We like it over baked potatoes. Variation: Use spinach, carrots, zucchini, green beans, peas, or mixed vegetables instead of broccoli. Energy-saving tip: This recipe can be doubled for a large group, or halved for a single meal and browned in the toaster oven while a baked potato cooks in the microwave.

INGREDIENTS

1	pkg. (10 oz.) frozen broccoli	1	can (4 oz.) sliced mushrooms, with liquid
2	Tbsp. reduced-calorie margarine	2	cups (1 lb.) cooked chicken, sliced
2	Tbsp. flour	2	Tbsp. chopped parsley
1	cup homemade chicken broth	2	Tbsp. bread crumbs

METHOD

1. Cook broccoli according to package directions.
2. Mix margarine and flour together in saucepan. Cook briefly over medium heat. Blend in chicken broth, stirring constantly, until thickened and smooth. Sauce may be made in the microwave oven by combining ingredients and cooking on HIGH until thickened, stirring two or three times.
3. Stir in mushrooms and their liquid. Season to taste.
4. Place broccoli pieces in shallow pan.
5. Cover with sliced chicken and pour mushroom sauce over all.
6. Top with parsley and bread crumbs.
7. Bake at 375° for 15–25 minutes, or until bubbly and brown on top.

⚖Balance with lower-fat dishes on days you use this recipe.

Lean Meat Exchange	3	Fat	9 grams (37%)
Vegetable Exchange	2	Saturated fat	2 grams
Calories	221	Cholesterol	64 milligrams
Carbohydrate	10 grams	Fiber	4 grams
Protein	25 grams	Sodium	258 milligrams

CHICKEN ROULADES WITH CURRY SAUCE

4 Servings/Serving size: 1/4 recipe

Save this for a special occasion such as Mother's Day luncheon or your best friend's birthday because it is time-consuming. It is an elegent presentation of familiar foods. All the trimmings and leftovers can be used to make chicken stock.

INGREDIENTS

4	4-oz. boneless, skinless chicken breast halves	8	broccoli spears
8	small spinach leaves, washed and trimmed	2	Tbsp. reduced-calorie mayonnaise
1/2	cup very fine carrot sticks, 1/8 x 1/8 x 2 inches	1	Tbsp. low-fat plain yogurt
1/2	cup leeks, cut same size as carrots	1/4	tsp. curry powder
	Freshly ground pepper to taste	2	dashes liquid red pepper sauce
		1/4	tsp. lemon juice
		1	large tomato, cut into 8 wedges
		16	small tender lettuce leaves

METHOD

1. Flatten chicken between sheets of wax paper to 5 x 6-inch rectangles, using a heavy skillet or mallet. Remove top sheet of wax paper.
2. Divide spinach evenly on top of chicken, leaving a 3/4-inch edge. Arrange carrot and leek on top of spinach; season with pepper.
3. Using the wax paper as a guide, roll chicken jelly-roll style. Secure each with string or toothpicks.
4. In a large saucepan or skillet, add water to a depth of 2 inches. Bring to a boil; lower heat; add chicken rolls and simmer 12–15 minutes, turning once. Reserve poaching liquid.
5. Wrap each roll in plastic wrap and chill.
6. Cook broccoli in poaching liquid for 3–5 minutes, or until tender-crisp. Chill.
7. In a small bowl combine mayonnaise, yogurt, curry, pepper sauce, and lemon juice until blended. Cut each chicken roll into 8 slices and arrange on plates with lettuce, broccoli, and tomato wedges; pass sauce separately.

Lean Meat Exchange	3	Fat	5 grams (26%)
Vegetable Exchange	2	Saturated fat	1 gram
Calories	173	Cholesterol	79 milligrams
Carbohydrate	9 grams	Fiber	4 grams
Protein	23 grams	Sodium	194 milligrams

GLAZED CHICKEN WITH VEGETABLES*

8 Servings/Serving size: 1/8 recipe

This one-pot meal was a hit at a four-generation taste test. Everyone from 4 to 84 voted for it. Serve with a light salad and some crusty bread. Energy-saving tip: Make enough for another meal. Reheat as is in the microwave oven. A little more broth or water may be needed for top of range heating.

INGREDIENTS

3–4	lb. chicken parts, skin and fat removed	2	Tbsp. lemon juice
3	Tbsp. corn oil	1	can (8 oz.) mushrooms with liquid
1/2	tsp. salt (optional)	1/2–1	cup homemade chicken broth, divided
1/4	tsp. pepper		
2	Tbsp. flour	1/2	cup dry red wine
1	tsp. sugar	2	lb. small onions, peeled
1/4	tsp. thyme	1	lb. carrots, peeled, quartered, and cut into 2-inch chunks
1/4	tsp. rosemary		

METHOD

1. In large heavy kettle, brown chicken in oil, salt, and pepper. Remove chicken.
2. Stir flour, sugar, thyme, and rosemary into drippings until smooth.
3. Add lemon juice, mushroom juice, and 1/2 cup chicken broth, stirring until it boils.
4. Add wine, onions, carrots, mushrooms, and chicken. Cover and simmer until vegetables are almost tender, about 20–30 minutes, adding more chicken broth if needed to keep food from sticking.
5. Remove cover; stir and continue cooking at slightly higher heat until most of the liquid is gone and chicken and vegetables are coated with a thick glaze.

*Not recommended for low-sodium diets if salt is added.

Starch/Bread Exchange	1	Fat	12 grams (30%)
Lean Meat Exchange	5	Saturated fat	2 grams
Vegetable Exchange	2	Cholesterol	107 milligrams
Calories	364	Fiber	3 grams
Carbohydrate	19 grams	Sodium	420 milligrams
Protein	45 grams	Without added salt	276 milligrams

PITA SANDWICH

4 Servings/Serving size: 1 sandwich

Pita breads are available in the deli section of most supermarkets. They come in various sizes and flavors. I prefer the whole-wheat ones. Especially good with chicken picked off the bones from making chicken stock.

INGREDIENTS

2	6-inch whole-wheat pitas		Herbed Yogurt:
4	oz. cooked chicken, slivered	1/2	cup low-fat plain yogurt
1	ripe tomato, thinly sliced	1/4	cup cucumber, diced or grated
1	small cucumber, slivered or grated	1	clove garlic, minced
		1	Tbsp. white vinegar
1/2	cup herbed yogurt	1	Tbsp. fresh mint, chopped, or 1 tsp. dried

METHOD

1. Combine Herbed Yogurt ingredients. Chill to allow flavors to blend. (May also be used as a dip or salad dressing.)
2. Heat pitas. Cut in half crosswise and pull apart to make pockets.
3. Divide the chicken, tomato, and cucumber evenly and place in the four pita pockets.
4. Top with herbed yogurt. Garnish with dried oregano.

With Herbed Yogurt:

Starch/Bread Exchange	2	Fat	4 grams (19%)
Lean Meat Exchange	2	Saturated fat	trace
Calories	192	Cholesterol	34 milligrams
Carbohydrate	23 grams	Fiber	1 gram
Protein	16 grams	Sodium	221 milligrams

TURKEY AND NOODLES WITH POPPY SEEDS

12 Servings/Serving size: 1 cup

A big, hearty casserole that can be halved, doubled, frozen, or reheated. Energy-saving tip: Cook noodles the energy-saving way. Bring water to a rolling boil, add noodles. Stir and bring to boil again. Cover. Turn heat off. Let stand for recommended cooking time. Stir and drain.

INGREDIENTS

1	pkg. (8 oz.) wide noodles (or use the homemade noodles in the BREAD section)	1/4	tsp. pepper
		1/2	tsp. salt (optional)
		1/2	lb. soft tofu, mashed
1 1/2 lb. turkey, ground		1	cup nonfat ricotta cheese
1	medium onion, chopped	1/2	cup low-fat plain yogurt
1	small green pepper, chopped	1	Tbsp. poppy seed
1	can (15 oz.) tomato sauce		

METHOD

1. Start cooking the noodles. While they are cooking, cook the turkey, onions, and green pepper in large skillet, until turkey is no longer pink.
2. Stir in tomato sauce, salt, and pepper.
3. Combine cheeses, yogurt, poppy seed, and noodles.
4. Spread 3/4 of the noodle mixture in a 13 x 9 x 2 inch baking dish. Top with meat mixture, leaving a 1-inch border of uncovered noodles.
5. Spread the rest of the noodle mixture in the center of the pan leaving a 1-inch meat border.
6. Bake covered at 375° for 30 minutes. Uncover and bake 10–15 minutes longer or until the casserole is heated through.

⚖ Balance with lower-fat dishes on days you use this recipe.

Starch/Bread Exchange	1	Saturated fat	2 grams
Medium-Fat Meat Exchange	2	Cholesterol	40 milligrams
Calories	245	Fiber	1 gram
Carbohydrate	21 grams	Sodium	170 milligrams
Protein	20 grams	Without added salt	73 milligrams
Fat	9 grams (33%)		

TURKEY SAUSAGE SCRAMBLE*

6 Servings/Serving size: 1 cup

This is a great brunch dish. It is tasty when first made, it can sit around on low heat for a while, and leftovers reheat well in the microwave. Use 50% power for reheating. This goes together fast so have everything ready to use when you start cooking.

INGREDIENTS

1   lb. raw turkey sausage
1   large onion, chopped
1 1/2 cups egg substitute
1   can (16 oz.) cream-style corn

METHOD

1. Cut each sausage into 4 pieces (use kitchen shears if you have them).
2. Saute sausage and onions until sausage is no longer pink inside and onions are soft. A nonstick skillet works best for this.
3. Add the corn and egg substitute and scramble until set. It is ready to serve.

 Balance with lower-fat dishes on days you use this recipe. *Not recommended for low-sodium diets.

Starch/Bread Exchange	1	Fat	10 grams (38%)
Medium-Fat Meat Exchange	2	Saturated fat	4 grams
Vegetable Exchange	1	Cholesterol	46 milligrams
Calories	238	Fiber	2 grams
Carbohydrate	16 grams	Sodium	728 milligrams
Protein	21 grams		

FRIED RICE WITH CRABMEAT

6 Servings/Serving size: 1/6 recipe

A low-calorie, low-fat version. Great as part of a buffet supper.

INGREDIENTS

1 1/4	cups brown rice
1	Tbsp. corn oil
4	scallions, sliced or 1/2 cup onions, chopped
1	clove garlic, minced
7	oz. crabmeat
4	oz. canned bamboo shoots, cut into matchstick strips
2	Tbsp. lite soy sauce.

METHOD

1. Boil rice according to the package directions; set aside for several hours to dry out completely.
2. Heat oil in a large saucepan; stir-fry onions and garlic for 1–2 minutes.
3. Add rice and stir-fry until heated through.
4. Add remaining ingredients and stir-fry until very hot.
5. Remove from heat. Keep in a warm oven until ready to serve.

Lean Meat Exchange	1	Fat	4 grams (17%)
Starch/Bread Exchange	2	Saturated fat	trace
Calories	208	Cholesterol	29 milligrams
Carbohydrate	32 grams	Fiber	3 grams
Protein	11 grams	Sodium	140 milligrams

SALMON STEAK WITH CUCUMBER SAUCE

2 Servings/Serving size: 1 steak with 2 Tbsp. sauce

This recipe may be doubled easily.

INGREDIENTS

1	cup water
1	Tbsp. lemon juice
2	(4-oz.) single-serving–size salmon steaks
1/4	cup cucumber, finely chopped
1/4	cup nonfat plain yogurt
1	tsp. minced parsley
1/4	tsp. dried dill or 1 tsp. fresh dill, chopped
1/4	tsp. grated onion or 1/2 tsp. dried onion flakes
1/2	tsp. lemon juice
	Freshly ground black pepper
6	tender lettuce leaves
2	lemon wedges

METHOD

1. Heat water and lemon juice to boiling. Add salmon in single layer. Simmer very gently for 10 minutes. Or microwave salmon in covered casserole, thickest part of fish toward the outside. Microwave on HIGH for 3 1/2 minutes and let stand 3 minutes.
2. Remove salmon with slotted spatula. Cover and chill.
3. Combine cucumber, yogurt, parsley, dill, onion, lemon juice, and pepper.
4. Arrange salmon on lettuce. Serve with lemon wedges and cucumber sauce.

⚖ Balance with lower-fat dishes on days you use this recipe.

Medium-Fat Meat Exchange 3	Saturated fat................................1 gram
Calories 146	Cholesterol.......................49 milligrams
Carbohydrate ....4 grams	Fiber ....1 gram
Protein ....19 grams	Sodium............................64 milligrams
Fat...................................6 grams (37%)	

SALMON AND WHITE BEAN SALAD*

4 Servings/Serving size: 1/4 recipe

The chief ingredients come right off the shelf, a boon for long-range shoppers and handy for last-minute meals.

INGREDIENTS

2   scallions, sliced, or a handful of fresh chives from the garden, chopped

1   can (16 oz.) small white cooked beans, drained

1   can (7 1/2 oz.) red salmon, drained and separated into chunks

1   stalk celery, thinly sliced

12 tender lettuce leaves

1   Tbsp. Vinaigrette dressing

Vinaigrette Dressing:

2   Tbsp. wine vinegar

2   Tbsp. olive oil

1/4 tsp. each salt, sugar, and dry mustard

Freshly ground pepper

METHOD

1. Combine dressing ingredients. Stir or shake in jar.
2. Combine scallions or chives, beans, salmon, celery, and dressing.
3. Arrange on lettuce-lined plates.

*Not recommended for low-sodium diets.

With 1 Tbsp. dressing:

Starch/Bread Exchange	1
Medium-Fat Meat Exchange	2
Fat Exchange	2
Calories	218
Carbohydrate	18 grams
Protein	14 grams
Fat	10 grams (41%)
Saturated fat	1.5 grams
Cholesterol	18 milligrams
Fiber	9 grams
Sodium	845 milligrams

FISH FOR TWO FROM THE MICROWAVE

2 Servings/Serving size: 4 oz.

Faster than fast-food take-out! And a lot fewer calories. Also try cooking fish this way when you want plain poached or steamed fish for some other recipe. Variations: Top fish with fresh chopped tomatoes and basil; sprinkle with salt-free seasoning; season with pepper. Dip in skim milk or water and coat with cornflake crumbs. May need to add up to a minute cooking time. Cover with paper towel before cooking.

INGREDIENTS

1/2   lb. fish fillets
1/2   fresh lemon

METHOD

1. Arrange fish with the thickest portion in the outer edge of the dish. Cover.
2. Microwave 2 1/2–3 minutes on HIGH or until fish flakes. Let stand 3 minutes, covered. Microwave lemon 20 seconds on HIGH. Squeeze over fish.

Lean Meat Exchange.............................4
Calories 126
Carbohydrate..............................1 gram
Protein ....26 grams
Fat...............................2 grams (14%)

Saturated fat .... trace
Cholesterol.........................48 milligrams
Fiber..0 grams
Sodium.............................71 milligrams

LOW-CALORIE FISH FILLETS FOR FOUR

4 Servings/Serving size: 4 oz.

There will be some tasty juices that go well on rice or potatoes.

INGREDIENTS

1	lb. fish fillets
1	medium onion, thinly sliced
1/2–1 cup sliced mushrooms
1	large tomato, sliced
	Salt and pepper or Mrs. Dash seasoning
1	Tbsp. lemon juice
2	Tbsp. reduced-calorie margarine

METHOD

1. Place fish in microwave casserole, arranging thicker portion toward the outside.
2. Layer vegetables over fish. Sprinkle with seasonings, lemon juice, and margarine.
3. Cover. Microwave on HIGH 3 minutes. Rotate dish if necessary and microwave on HIGH 3 minutes more. Let stand 3 minutes.

Lean Meat Exchange................................4	Fat.....................................4 grams (22%)
Vegetable Exchange................................1	Saturated fat.........................1 milligram
Calories...164	Cholesterol.........................48 milligrams
Carbohydrate..............................5 grams	Fiber..1 gram
Protein..27 grams	Sodium............................129 milligrams

SCALLOPS AND BRAISED RED ONIONS

4 Servings/Serving size: 1/4 recipe

Delectable enough to serve to your most discriminating guest and to your favorite scallop enthusiast. Serve with a side dish of potatoes and a crunchy salad.

INGREDIENTS

1 1/2 lb.	red onions, thinly sliced
1	Tbsp. corn oil
1/3	cup water
2	tsp. sugar
2	tsp. lemon juice
	Freshly ground black pepper
1	lb. scallops, cut in half if very large (12 oz. cooked)
1	clove garlic or 1/2 tsp. dried garlic, minced
2	Tbsp. (1 oz.) dry vermouth

METHOD

1. Saute onions in nonstick pan in hot oil until onions begin to soften (10 minutes over medium-high heat).
2. Add water and sugar and partially cover. Cook over low heat until water evaporates.
3. Sprinkle with lemon juice and pepper.
4. Add scallops and garlic. Saute for several minutes until scallops are cooked.
5. Stir in vermouth and cook quickly for 30 seconds.

Lean Meat Exchange	3	Fat	6 grams (26%)
Starch/Bread Exchange	1	Saturated fat	1 gram
Calories	206	Cholesterol	38 milligrams
Carbohydrate	17 grams	Fiber	2 grams
Protein	21 grams	Sodium	200 milligrams

ORIENTAL STIR-FRY FISH AND VEGETABLES

5 Servings/Serving size: 1/5 recipe over 2/3 cup rice

This recipe is for colleagues who asked for a low-calorie meal they can put together from scratch after work.

INGREDIENTS

1	lb. white-fleshed fish, cut into 1-inch pieces	1/2	cup celery, sliced, 1/2 cup scallions, sliced
1/2	cup white wine	1	cup broccoli
1	tsp. ginger	1	cup cauliflowerets (or 1 bag (16 oz.) frozen, mixed Oriental vegetables)
1	tsp. garlic, dried or fresh, minced		
2	tsp. sugar	1	Tbsp. lite soy sauce
2	Tbsp. oil (use sesame oil if you have it for flavor)	1	tsp. cornstarch
2	cups mushrooms, sliced	3	cups hot cooked rice

METHOD

1. Make marinade by combining wine, ginger, garlic, sugar, and oil.
2. Marinate fish for at least 15 minutes.
3. Start cooking rice.
4. Saute the vegetables in a little of the marinade until partially cooked.
5. Add fish with the rest of the marinade and cook on medium heat until fish flakes.
6. Thicken sauce in pan with 1 tsp. of cornstarch dissolved in 1 Tbsp. soy sauce. Stir until sauce clears and thickens.
7. Serve over 2/3 cup cooked rice.

With rice:

Lean Meat Exchange	3	Protein	21 grams
Starch/Bread Exchange	2	Fat	7 grams (20%)
Vegetable Exchange	2	Saturated fat	1 gram
Calories	311	Cholesterol	36 milligrams
Carbohydrate	41 grams	Fiber	3 grams
		Sodium	91 milligrams

FISH AND FRUIT SALAD WITH YOGURT DRESSING

4 Servings/Serving size: 1/4 recipe

A light refreshing whole-meal salad or delightful addition to a buffet. Energy-saving tip: Save cooking liquid for fish chowder or something that calls for fish stock.

INGREDIENTS

1   lb. white fish, fresh or frozen
2   cups assorted fresh fruit (strawberries, grapes, and melon work well)
1/3   cup sliced celery
2   Tbsp. lite mayonnaise
1/3   cup low-fat lemon-flavored yogurt
2   scallions, thinly sliced
12   tender lettuce leaves

METHOD

1. Steam or poach fish until just cooked. It will be white all the way through and flake easily.
2. Drain well and chill. Flake into chunks.
3. Combine with fruit and celery.
4. Combine mayonnaise, yogurt, and onions. Pour over fish mixture and stir gently.
5. Refrigerate until ready to serve. Serve on lettuce.

Lean Meat Exchange..............................4	Fat......................................4 grams (19%)
Fruit Exchange 1	Saturated fat................................1 gram
Fat Exchange 1	Cholesterol.......................51 milligrams
Calories 192	Fiber...2 grams
Carbohydrate ....14 grams	Sodium...........................152 milligrams
Protein ....26 grams	

FISH FLORENTINE*

4 Servings/Serving size: 4 oz.

When I used to make this for microwave oven demonstrations, people said they tasted it out of curiosity but liked it so much that they made it at home for guests. Tips: The spinach can be cooked and the sauce prepared several hours ahead. Assemble with fish just before cooking. Thin fish fillets cook faster than thick pieces.

INGREDIENTS

1	pkg. (10 oz.) frozen chopped spinach	1/2	tsp. tarragon leaves
4	oz. fresh mushrooms, sliced	2	Tbsp. reduced-calorie margarine
1	lb. fish fillet	1	Tbsp. lemon juice
1	cup 1% milk	1/4	cup Parmesan cheese
2	Tbsp. flour		Paprika for color
1/2	tsp. salt		

METHOD

1. Microwave spinach in 1 1/2-qt. casserole 5–6 minutes on high. Drain.
2. Layer mushrooms and fish over spinach.
3. In bowl, combine milk, flour, salt, and tarragon, mixing well, and add margarine. Microwave 2–3 minutes on HIGH or until mixture boils and thickens, stirring once or twice.
4. Stir in lemon juice. Pour mixture over fish. Sprinkle with Parmesan cheese and paprika.
5. Cover. Microwave 7–10 minutes on HIGH or until fish flakes with fork.

*Not recommended for low-sodium diets if salt is added.

Lean Meat Exchange	4	Fat	6 grams (27%)
Vegetable Exchange	2	Saturated fat	2 grams
Fat Exchange	1	Cholesterol	55 milligrams
Calories	198	Fiber	3 grams
Carbohydrate	9 grams	Sodium	570 milligrams
Protein	27 grams	Without added salt	283 milligrams

HALIBUT WITH A GREEK FLAVOR*

6 Servings/Serving size: 1/6 recipe

A colorful way to serve the lovely halibut that has been showing up at fish counters. Serve with orzo (a small oval-shaped pasta), rice, or baked potato.

INGREDIENTS

1 1/2 lb.	fresh or frozen halibut steaks, thawed, 3/4 inch thick
2	Tbsp. reduced-calorie margarine
1/4	cup egg substitute
1/3	cup skim milk
1	cup feta cheese, crumbled
1/8	tsp. ground red pepper
1	large tomato, chopped
1/4	cup pitted black olives, chopped
1/4	cup pine nuts or slivered almonds
1	Tbsp. lemon juice
	Freshly ground pepper

METHOD

1. Cut halibut into 6 portions. Saute in margarine over medium-high heat for about 3 minutes each side. Place in single layer in baking dish.
2. Combine egg substitute, milk, cheese, and red pepper; pour over halibut.
3. Scatter tomato, olives, and nuts over top. Bake at 400° for 10 minutes.
4. Sprinkle with lemon juice, parsley, and pepper.

⚖ Balance with lower-fat dishes on days you use this recipe. *Not recommended for low-sodium diets.

Lean Meat Exchange............................5	Fat.................................17 grams (51%)
Fat Exchange 1	Saturated fat................................7 grams
Calories...301	Cholesterol........................69 milligrams
Carbohydrate.........................5 grams	Fiber...1 gram
Protein..................................32 grams	Sodium............................627 milligrams

MYSTERY FISH DISH

4 Servings/Serving size: 1/4 recipe

Taste testers liked this but could not identify the vegetable part. It is a real taste treat when you are looking for something out of the ordinary.

INGREDIENTS

1	Tbsp. reduced-calorie margarine
2	tsp. curry powder
1	medium onion, thinly sliced
3	cups green cabbage, finely shredded
3/4	lb. boneless salmon, skinned and cut into 2-inch chunks
1/2	tsp. salt (optional)
1/4	tsp. freshly ground pepper
1	tsp. lemon juice

METHOD

1. Spray casserole dish with nonstick vegetable cooking spray. Melt margarine in covered casserole. Add curry powder, onion, and cabbage; stir to coat. Cover and microwave on HIGH for 4 minutes.
2. Stir. Mound cabbage in center of dish and arrange salmon around cabbage.
3. Sprinkle with salt, pepper, and lemon juice. Cover and microwave on HIGH for 8 minutes.
4. Stir. Replace cover and let stand for 3 minutes.

⚖ Balance with lower-fat dishes on days you use this recipe.

Lean Meat Exchange................................3	Saturated fat ....2 grams
Vegetable Exchange 1	Cholesterol.......................32 milligrams
Calories 167	Fiber ....1 gram
Carbohydrate ....7 grams	Sodium...........................367 milligrams
Protein ....19 grams	Without added salt............79 milligrams
Fat...................................7 grams (38%)	

STIR-FRY SCALLOPS AND BROCCOLI

3 Servings/Serving size: 1/3 recipe

I tried not to have favorites when testing the recipes for this book but could not help it when I tried this. It was just as good when the recipe was doubled for a Sunday brunch.

INGREDIENTS

1/2	lb. scallops, cut in half if very large (6 oz. cooked)
2	Tbsp. cornstarch, divided
3	Tbsp. lite soy sauce, divided
1	tsp. sugar
1/2	tsp. ground ginger
1	cup water
1/4	tsp. minced garlic
1/2	lb. fresh broccoli, cut into serving pieces
1	medium onion, cubed
2	medium carrots, sliced diagonally
	Freshly ground black pepper

METHOD

1. Mix the scallops with 1 Tbsp. each cornstarch and soy sauce. Let stand 10–15 minutes.
2. Combine remaining cornstarch, soy sauce, sugar, and ginger with the water.
3. Saute scallop mixture in nonstick skillet.
4. Add vegetables. Cook and stir for several minutes.
5. Add water mixture and pepper. Cook until sauce thickens and vegetables are tender-crisp.

Lean Meat Exchange	2	Fat	1 grams (6%)
Vegetable Exchange	1	Saturated fat	trace
Starch/Bread Exchange	1	Cholesterol	25 milligrams
Calories	153	Fiber	1 gram
Carbohydrate	20 grams	Sodium	228 milligrams
Protein	16 grams		

SCALLOPS, PEPPERS, AND PASTA

6 Servings/Serving size: 1/6 recipe

A flavorful way to stretch a pound of scallops to 6 servings.

INGREDIENTS

1/2	lb. pasta spirals or rounds
1	lb. sea scallops, cut in half if very large (12 oz. cooked) Flour for dredging
3/4	cup homemade chicken or fish stock, divided
1	large onion, chopped
1	small red sweet pepper, cut into strips
1	small green pepper, cut into strips
1/2	lb. fresh mushrooms, sliced
1/2	cup tomato sauce
1	tsp. fennel seed

METHOD

1. Cook pasta the energy saving way by bringing water to a rolling boil, adding pasta, stirring until boils again. Cover. Remove from heat. Let stand for cooking time on package. Drain.
2. Dredge scallops in flour.
3. Heat 1/4 cup of stock in large skillet over medium heat. Add onions and cook until translucent.
4. Add peppers and mushrooms and cook until some of the liquid has evaporated.
5. Add the scallops and cook, stirring, until scallops are opaque, about 5 minutes.
6. Add tomato sauce, fennel, and 1/2 cup chicken stock. Bring to a boil and then reduce heat to simmer for 1–2 minutes.
7. Serve scallops over pasta.

Lean Meat Exchange	2	Fat	1 gram (4%)
Vegetable Exchange	2	Saturated fat	trace
Starch/Bread Exchange	1	Cholesterol	25 milligrams
Calories	197	Fiber	4 grams
Carbohydrate	33 grams	Sodium	242 milligrams
Protein	14 grams		

VEAL SCALLOPINI WITH SPINACH NOODLES*

6 Servings/Serving size: 1/6 recipe

This dish can be made at several budget levels. The most exquisite (and expensive) uses veal cutlets, fresh spinach fettucini, and capers. A more modest approach uses boneless chicken breast when it is on sale, dried spinach noodles, and no capers. Serve with a simply-prepared fresh vegetable in season or microwave something frozen. And have a colorful salad. Dessert could be the Chocolate Log from the DESSERT section with freshly brewed coffee.

INGREDIENTS

6	oz. fettucini noodles	1	can (16 oz.) tomatoes, cut up
3	Tbsp. flour	1	can (3 oz.) sliced mushrooms
1	tsp. salt (optional)		with liquid
1/4	tsp. pepper	1	Tbsp. parsley, snipped
6	veal cutlets (1 1/2 lb.) or	1	Tbsp. capers, drained
	equivalent amount of boneless		(optional)
	chicken breast	1/4	tsp. garlic, minced
1	Tbsp. corn oil	1/4	tsp. oregano
1	cup onions, coarsely chopped		Sprig of parsley

METHOD

1. Prepare fettucini according to package directions.
2. Combine flour, salt, and pepper. Dredge meat and sauté in hot oil in heavy skillet.
3. Remove meat, add onions, and cook until tender. Do not brown.
4. Return meat to pot. Stir in tomatoes, undrained mushrooms, parsley, capers, garlic, and oregano.
5. Cover and simmer 20 minutes or until meat is tender, stirring occasionally.
6. Arrange meat in center of platter. Spoon some sauce over meat. If sauce is too thin, thicken with about 2 tsp. of cornstarch mixed with 2 Tbsp. of cold water.
7. Add cooked fettucini to rest of the sauce and heat through. Arrange fettucini around meat. Garnish with sprig of parsley.

*Not recommended for low-sodium diets if salt is added.

Starch/Bread Exchange	2	Fat	12 grams (30%)
Lean Meat Exchange	3	Saturated fat	4 grams
Vegetable Exchange	1	Cholesterol	104 milligrams
Calories	340	Fiber	2 grams
Carbohydrate	31 grams	Sodium	643 milligrams
Protein	27 grams	Without added salt	259 milligrams

PIQUANT MEAT LOAF

10 Servings/Serving size: 1 slice with 2 tsp. sauce

This is my family's favorite meat loaf, always cooked as part of an oven meal along with baked or scalloped potatoes, a vegetable such as carrots or turnips in a covered casserole, and apple crisp or some kind of fruit dessert. Always, that is, until the microwave oven came along. Now I make meat loaf whether I want the rest of the oven meal or not. We like meat loaf with potato salad and hope there is enough left for sandwiches the next day.

INGREDIENTS

1 1/2	lb. ground beef or turkey
2/3	cup rolled oats
2/3	cup skim milk (use 3/4 cup with turkey)
1/2	cup egg substitute
1	small onion, chopped
1/2–1	tsp. salt (optional)
1/8	tsp. pepper (use a little more with turkey)
1/2	tsp. sage (use 3/4 tsp. with turkey)

Piquant Sauce:

3	Tbsp. brown sugar or sugar substitute
1/4	cup catsup
1/4	tsp. nutmeg (use 1/3 tsp. with turkey)
1	tsp. dry mustard (use 1 1/4 tsp. with turkey)

METHOD

1. Combine all meatloaf ingredients and mix thoroughly. Press into microwave ring mold or make your own by putting a custard cup in the center of a large, round casserole and packing the meat loaf around the edges.
2. Combine sauce ingredients and spread over top of meat loaf.
3. Microwave 12–14 minutes on HIGH.
4. Let stand 10 minutes before serving.

⚖ Balance with lower-fat dishes on days you use this recipe.

Starch/Bread Exchange	1	Saturated fat	3 grams
Lean Meat Exchange	2	Cholesterol	35 milligrams
Calories	172	Fiber	trace
Carbohydrate	11 grams	Sodium	302 milligrams
Protein	14 grams	Without added salt	130 milligrams
Fat	8 grams (42%)		

INDIVIDUAL MEAT LOAF

1 Serving

Variations: Add green pepper or top with tomato or barbecue sauce. A thick, spicy topping is especially tasty with mild-flavored turkey.

INGREDIENTS

1/4	lb. lean ground beef or turkey
3	Tbsp. rolled oats or bread crumbs
2	Tbsp. skim milk
1	Tbsp. onion, diced, or 1 tsp. dried onion flakes
1/2	tsp. Worcestershire sauce
1/4	tsp. pepper

METHOD

1. Mix all ingredients thoroughly. Press into a microwave-safe flat-bottomed bowl.
2. Microwave on MEDIUM HIGH (70% power) for 3–3 1/2 minutes or until meat is firm. Let stand 2 minutes.

⚖ Balance with lower-fat dishes on days you use this recipe.

Starch/Bread Exchange	1	Fat	11 grams (41%)
Lean Meat Exchange	3	Saturated fat	4 grams
Calories	239	Cholesterol	53 milligrams
Carbohydrate	16 grams	Fiber	trace
Protein	19 grams	Sodium	221 milligrams

SLOPPY JOES*

6 Servings/Serving Size: 1 sandwich

When browning meat in the microwave oven for use in spaghetti or a casserole, place the meat in a microwave-safe plastic colander. Set the colander in a bowl and microwave. The fat will drain from the meat and collect in the bowl, reducing the amount of fat to be eaten. Refrigerate the drippings, lift off the congealed fat, and use the juice in soups and sauces. Variations: Add 1 cup (4 oz.) shredded cheese (soy mozzarella has less cholesterol than cow's milk cheese) or add baked beans or red kidney beans and heat a little longer.

INGREDIENTS
1 1/2 lb. lean ground beef or turkey
2/3 cup onion, chopped
1/2 cup celery, chopped
1/2 cup green pepper, chopped
1/2 cup catsup
1 Tbsp. Worcestershire sauce
1/4 tsp. salt (optional)
1/8 tsp. pepper
1 hamburger roll per serving

METHOD
1. Microwave crumbled meat, onions, celery, and green pepper on HIGH for 6 minutes, stirring twice. Drain.
2. Add rest of ingredients. Stir well.
3. Cover. Microwave on HIGH for 5–6 minutes until hot.
4. Stir. Spoon onto buns or crusty rolls.

*Not recommended for low-sodium diets.

Starch/Bread Exchange......................2	Fat.............................11 grams (30%)
Lean Meat Exchange...........................3	Saturated fat...........................4.3 grams
Vegetable Exchange..............................1	Cholesterol.......................55 milligrams
Calories...335	Fiber..1 gram
Carbohydrate.........................38 grams	Sodium..........................672 milligrams
Protein......................................21 grams	Without added salt.........576 milligrams

ONE-POT PORK CHOP DINNER*

4 Servings/Serving size: 1 chop

Use a large heavy skillet with cover or a Dutch oven for this. Multiply or divide ingredients to fit your needs. Serve with crusty bread and a vegetable salad. How about a baked apple for dessert? See DESSERT section for microwave instructions.

INGREDIENTS

4	(3-oz.) meaty, center-cut pork chops, 3/4-inch thick
1/4	cup flour
2	tsp. paprika
1/2	tsp. salt (optional)
1/4	tsp. pepper
1	large or 2 medium onions, thickly sliced
1 1/2–2 cups skim milk	
1	large stalk (about 1 lb.) broccoli

METHOD

1. Trim fat from chops and fry in skillet over medium-high heat.
2. Combine flour, paprika, salt, and pepper and coat chops. (Save remaining flour.) Brown chops in skillet. Coat onions with remaining flour and add to skillet. Brown lightly.
3. Add 1 1/2 cups milk. Bring to boil, cover and simmer for 20 minutes, stirring occasionally. If sauce is too thick, add more milk.
4. Peel broccoli stalk if tough, cut into slices, and add to skillet. Place florets on top. Cover and simmer until broccoli and pork are tender.

*Not recommended for low-sodium diets if salt is added.

Starch/Bread Exchange	1	Fat	10 grams (30%)
Medium-Fat Meat Exchange	4	Saturated fat	3 grams
Vegetable Exchange	1	Cholesterol	86 milligrams
Calories	290	Fiber	1 gram
Carbohydrate	17 grams	Sodium	431 milligrams
Protein	33 grams	Without added salt	143 milligrams

6 Servings/Serving size: 1/6 recipe

You may have to plan ahead for the lamb for this dish, if you live in a small village as I do. But this one-pot meal is so easy and delicious that it is worth the extra planning. Serving suggestion: Fresh vegetables with a dip instead of a regular salad, and cookies from the DESSERT section.

INGREDIENTS

2	lb. lamb, cut into 2-inch cubes
1/4	cup flour
1/2	tsp. salt (optional)
1/4	tsp. pepper
1	can (10 1/2 oz.) beef broth
2	medium green peppers, cubed
1/2	tsp. marjoram
3	cloves garlic, minced
1	lb. new potatoes, scrubbed and a thin strip of peel removed
2	medium onions, sliced
1	cup celery, sliced
2	ripe tomatoes, cut in wedges
1/4	cup stuffed olives, sliced

METHOD

1. Use a large, heavy kettle with cover. Dredge meat with a mixture of flour, salt, and pepper. Brown lamb in nonstick vegetable cooking spray.
2. Add beef broth, green peppers, marjoram, and garlic. Cover and cook over low heat for 30 minutes, stirring occasionally.
3. Add potatoes, onions, and celery. Cook until vegetables are tender.
4. Stir in tomatoes and olives. Cover. Turn burner off and finish heating with reserved heat.

*Not recommended for low-sodium diets if salt is added.

Starch/Bread Exchange	1	Saturated fat	3 grams
Meat Exchange	4	Cholesterol	53 milligrams
Calories	269	Fiber	3 grams
Carbohydrate	19 grams	Sodium	535 milligrams
Protein	28 grams	Without added salt	343 milligrams
Fat	9 grams (30%)		

STUFFED ACORN SQUASH

4 Servings/Serving size: 1/4 recipe

Squash is handsome growing in the garden or piled up at the farmer's market. Here's a way to feature fresh acorn squash. Make this filling or use leftover Sloppy Joe mix or Chili Con Carne. Another vegetable would go nicely with this, such as Zesty Stir-Fried Spinach or Mushroom Asparagus Casserole, both in the VEGETABLE section. And Naturally Sweetened Date Bread from the BREAD section could double as dessert.

INGREDIENTS

2	medium acorn squash (about 1 lb. each)
3/4	lb. ground beef or turkey
1	small onion, diced
1	cup nonfat mozzarella, shredded
1/4	cup catsup
1/2	tsp. sugar
	Pepper to taste

METHOD

1. Cut squash in half, lengthwise. Remove seeds. Cook squash in 1/2-inch deep water in covered skillet (I use the electric skillet). This takes about 10 minutes. Drain liquid from squash cavities.
2. Meanwhile, brown meat and onion in saucepan, stir in rest of ingredients. Turn off heat and use heat in burner to finish heating mixture, stirring frequently.
3. To serve, place squash cut side up on plates; sprinkle lightly with pepper if desired. Spoon meat mixture into squash centers.

Starch/Bread Exchange	1	Fat	8 grams (29%)
Lean Meat Exchange	4	Saturated fat	3 grams
Calories	252	Cholesterol	44 milligrams
Carbohydrate	17 grams	Fiber	1 gram
Protein	28 grams	Sodium	187 milligrams

GUIDELINES FOR MICROWAVING VEGETABLES

Little, if any, water must be added when cooking vegetables. Often enough moisture clings to the vegetable from washing; otherwise just one or two tablespoons of water is usually enough. Very few nutrients are lost when vegetables are microwaved, because the water-soluble nutrients do not have a chance to leach out into cooking water.

Cover vegetables tightly; it speeds cooking, food cooks more evenly, and less water is needed.

Pierce skins of potatoes, winter squash, egg yolks, chicken, apples, and anything else that has a solid skin. Holes in the skin keep food from exploding due to steam buildup.

Arrange tender parts such as asparagus tips and broccoli florets toward the center of the dish, where they will get less heat than at the outer edges.

Vegetable pieces of uniform size and thickness cook more evenly than uneven pieces.

Frozen vegetables are almost fully cooked and may require less time than fresh vegetables. Packaged frozen vegetables can be cooked right in the carton or pouch if there is no foil or wire on the package. Cut an X in the top of a waxed box of vegetables, place carton on plate or paper towel. Allow a few minutes standing time after cooking. Cut a large X across a plastic pouch, place X down on a plate, and microwave. Once it is cooked, pick up two corners and the food will fall out onto the plate.

Canned vegetables need only to be warmed as they are already cooked. Save the vegetable water for soups.

To season vegetables:
Top with fresh lemon wedges and squeeze.
Try nutmeg on spinach, a touch of oregano with zucchini, basil with tomatoes, and dill or parsley with potatoes.
Sprinkle with salt-free seasonings.

SUMMER VEGETABLE KABOBS

8 Servings/Serving size: 1 kabob

This recipe makes enough kabobs for 8 servings, and I recommend making the entire batch even if you need fewer kabobs because the leftovers make perfectly wonderful stir-fry fixings. Just put marinade and all into a nonstick pan over medium-high heat, and they are ready in a few minutes either as a vegetable side dish or hot hors d'oeuvres (set out the toothpicks for spearing hors d'oeuvres).

INGREDIENTS

1	8-inch yellow squash	1/4	tsp. marjoram
1	8-inch zucchini	1	small bay leaf, crumbled
1	small firm eggplant	1	clove garlic, minced
8	small white onions	1	Tbsp. snipped fresh parsley
1	Tbsp. corn oil	1	sweet red pepper, cut into 8
2	Tbsp. fresh lemon juice		squares
1	Tbsp. red wine vinegar	1	green pepper, cut into 8
1 1/2 tsp. Dijon mustard			squares
1/2	tsp. basil	8	mushrooms
1/4	tsp. thyme	8	cherry tomatoes

METHOD

1. Cut the squash and zucchini into 16 slices each. Cut the eggplant into 1-inch cubes. Peel onions.
2. In a large container with cover, combine oil, 5 Tbsp. cold water, lemon juice, vinegar, mustard, basil, thyme, marjoram, bay leaf, garlic, and parsley.
3. Add the vegetables. Stir to coat. Cover and marinate in refrigerator at least 2 hours or overnight. Stir occasionally.
4. To grill, remove vegetables from marinade and thread onto skewers.
5. Place on heated grill. Brush with reserved marinade, turning often until vegetables are tender-crisp, about 10–12 minutes.

Vegetable Exchange	2	Saturated fat	trace
Calories	66	Cholesterol	0 milligrams
Carbohydrate	10 grams	Fiber	3 grams
Protein	2 grams	Sodium	24 milligrams
Fat	2 grams (27%)		

MUSHROOM-ASPARAGUS CASSEROLE

6 Servings/Serving size: 1/6 recipe

Substitute any vegetable you wish for the asparagus.

INGREDIENTS

1/2	lb. mushrooms, sliced
2	Tbsp. reduced-calorie margarine
4	Tbsp. flour
2	cups skim milk
1/4	tsp. minced onion
1	can (15 oz.) asparagus or 2 pkg. (10 oz. each) frozen thawed asparagus or equivalent in another vegetable, drained and cut into bite-size pieces
1	cup seasoned stuffing mix

METHOD

1. Saute mushrooms briefly in melted margarine. Remove from skillet.
2. Add flour to skillet and blend thoroughly.
3. Add milk gradually and cook, stirring constantly, until mixture thickens. Add seasonings and vegetables.
4. Pour into casserole coated with nonstick vegetable cooking spray.
5. Top with stuffing mix. Bake until bubbly at 350° for about 20 minutes.

Starch/Bread Exchange	1	Fat	3 grams (16%)
Vegetable Exchange	1	Saturated fat	trace
Fat Exchange	1/2	Cholesterol	1 milligram
Calories	167	Fiber	3 grams
Carbohydrate	26 grams	Sodium	142 milligrams
Protein	9 grams		

BROCCOLI, SWEET RED PEPPER, AND ORANGES

4 Servings/Serving size: 1/2 cup

Brunch and buffet suppers are a popular way to entertain family and friends. This dish is sure to be a colorful addition to any table.

INGREDIENTS

1/2	lb. broccoli florets
1	large or 2 small sweet red peppers, cut into strips
1	large or 2 small oranges
1/4	tsp. grated orange peel
1	tsp. sesame oil for flavor

METHOD

1. Microwave broccoli, red peppers, and 2 Tbsp. of water in covered casserole on HIGH for 6–8 minutes, until broccoli is tender-crisp, stirring once. Drain. Save juice for soup.
2. Peel and section oranges, saving juice. Add grated peel and oil to orange juice. Microwave on HIGH 20–30 seconds until bubbly.
3. Stir orange sections into broccoli/pepper mixture. Cook uncovered for 30 seconds or until heated through.
4. Drizzle with orange juice mixture.

Vegetable Exchange................................2	Saturated fat.......................................trace
Calories 53	Cholesterol,.........................0 milligrams
Carbohydrate ....9 grams	Fiber...4 grams
Protein ....2 grams	Sodium.............................14 milligrams
Fat.....................................1 gram (17%)	

HOT OR COLD CABBAGE

6 Servings/Serving size: 1 cup

Here's a job for the food processor. Makes 6 servings as a hot vegetable or more as a cold salad or relish. Good with baked beans.

INGREDIENTS

1/4	cup chicken broth
6	cups cabbage, finely shredded
1	cup carrot, coarsely grated
1	medium onion, chopped
2	cloves garlic, minced
1/4	cup catsup
1	tsp. hot pepper sauce
1/4	tsp. seasoning salt (optional)

METHOD

1. Heat broth in skillet with cover. Add vegetables and stir. Cover. Turn heat to medium-low and steam 5 minutes or until vegetables are tender-crisp, stirring several times. Turn heat off.
2. Add remaining ingredients and heat through with reserved heat.

Vegetable Exchange 2	Saturated fat ....0 grams
Calories 48	Cholesterol ....trace
Carbohydrate ....10 grams	Fiber ....1 gram
Protein ....2 grams	Sodium...........................282 milligrams
Fat ....0 grams (0%)	Without added salt..........186 milligrams

CARROTS WITH CORIANDER

4 Servings/Serving size: 1/2 cup

Carrots are full of flavor without any garnishes, but here's a way to make them company-special without too much fat or sodium.

INGREDIENTS

1	lb. carrots, sliced
1	tsp. vegetable oil
1	tsp. ground coriander
	Juice of 1/2 lemon
1/4	cup water
	Chopped fresh cilantro or parsley (as garnish)

METHOD

1. Saute carrots in oil in nonstick pan until golden.
2. Add coriander, lemon juice, and water. Bring to a boil and simmer until carrots are tender-crisp. Watch this carefully; carrots burn easily if the heat is too high.
3. Garnish.

Vegetable Exchange	1	Saturated fat	trace
Calories	45	Cholesterol	0 milligrams
Carbohydrate	7 grams	Fiber	1 gram
Protein	2 grams	Sodium	23 milligrams
Fat	1 gram (20%)		

BRAISED YELLOW ONIONS

4–6 Servings/Serving size: 1/2 cup

An incredibly delicious way to serve onions, with no fat at all. Remember this recipe when the supermarket has those 50-lb. specials or someone has a garden surplus. Turn on the exhaust fan over the range and move your peeling/slicing operation near the fan to cut down on eye irritation.

INGREDIENTS

1 1/2 lb. yellow onions, peeled and
      thinly sliced
1 1/2 pkgs. artificial sweetner
2   Tbsp. chicken broth
1/16 tsp. salt (optional)
4   whole cloves (optional)

METHOD

1. Combine all ingredients in a large, shallow baking dish.
2. Cover. Microwave on HIGH for 12 minutes. Serve hot.

Vegetable Exchange 1	Saturated fat ....0 grams
Calories 32	Cholesterol...........................0 milligrams
Carbohydrate ....7 grams	Fiber ....1 gram
Protein...1 gram	Sodium.............................75 milligrams
Fat ....0 grams (0%)	Without added salt...........46 milligrams

OVEN-FRIED ONION RINGS

4 Servings/Serving size: 1/2 cup (2 oz.)

Light and tasty treats that are particularly sweet with Vidalia onions but are good with whatever is available.

INGREDIENTS

1	large (8–10 oz.) sweet or Spanish-type onion
1	Tbsp. corn oil
2	Tbsp. cornmeal
2	Tbsp. fine bread crumbs
1	Tbsp. Parmesan cheese
1/8	tsp. paprika

METHOD

1. Peel onion; slice into 1/4 inch rings.
2. Sprinkle with oil and toss to coat.
3. Mix dry ingredients, sprinkle over onion rings, and toss to coat evenly.
4. Place on a nonstick baking sheet. Bake at 400° for 20 minutes or until lightly browned.

⚖ Balance with lower-fat dishes on days you use this recipe.

Vegetable Exchange	2	Fat	5 grams (48%)
Fat Exchange	1	Saturated fat	1 gram
Calories	93	Cholesterol	3 grams
Carbohydrate	9 grams	Fiber	1 gram
Protein	3 grams	Sodium	104 milligrams

ZIPPY POTATOES

4 Servings/Serving size: 1 potato

Some of you may have sampled this at a microwave oven demonstration. I've changed the recipe a little to make preparation easier and to create a more versatile dish using less fat than the original directions. This recipe makes 8–10 appetizers. Just provide toothpicks for spearing. These are also a nutritious snack for after school, after work, or anytime.

INGREDIENTS

4	medium potatoes, scrubbed but not peeled
1–2	onions (optional)
1	Tbsp. reduced-calorie margarine
1/2	tsp. garlic powder
1/2	tsp. paprika
2	Tbsp. Parmesan cheese

METHOD

1. Cut potatoes into long strips or bite-size pieces.
2. Cut onion into eighths.
3. Place vegetables in a shallow casserole or 8-inch-square pan. Dot vegetables with margarine. Sprinkle with seasonings.
4. Cover with paper towel. Microwave on HIGH for 8–10 minutes, stirring occasionally.

Starch/Bread Exchange	2	Fat	3 grams (17%)
Fat Exchange	1/2	Saturated fat	trace
Calories	159	Cholesterol	2 milligrams
Carbohydrate	28 grams	Fiber	3 grams
Protein	5 grams	Sodium	88 milligrams

4 Servings/Serving size: 1 potato

Good tasting French fries that are healthier and easier to make than the deep-fat–fried version.

INGREDIENTS

4	medium potatoes (about 1 1/2 pounds)
1	Tbsp. corn oil
	Paprika for color (optional)
1/2	oz. Parmesan cheese (optional)

METHOD

1. Wash potatoes, but do not peel. Cut into strips about 3/8 inch thick.
2. Spread oil in large, shallow baking pan.
3. Spread potatoes in pan and turn until evenly coated with oil.
4. Sprinkle with paprika. Bake at 475° for 25–30 minutes or until tender inside and golden brown, stirring and turning occasionally.
5. Sprinkle with Parmesan cheese.

Starch/Bread Exchange	1 1/2	Fat	4 grams (27%)
Fat Exchange	1	Saturated fat	1 gram
Calories	132	Cholesterol	2 milligrams
Carbohydrate	21 grams	Fiber	trace
Protein	3 grams	Sodium	53 milligrams

GARLIC POTATOES

4 Servings/Serving size: 2 potatoes

Small new potatoes are available from time to time. Here's a flavorful way to serve them. Leftovers may be reheated or used in salads.

INGREDIENTS

1	lb. (about 10) small new potatoes, scrubbed, patted dry, not peeled
6	large cloves garlic, peeled and smashed
2	Tbsp. olive oil
1/2	tsp. salt (optional)
	Freshly ground pepper

METHOD

1. Place all ingredients in microwave casserole. Stir to coat potatoes.
2. Cover. Microwave on HIGH for 10–15 minutes. Stir once or twice to rearrange potatoes. Check for doneness each time. Arrange least cooked potatoes around edge of the dish.
3. Serve hot.

Starch/Bread Exchange 2
Fat Exchange 1
Calories 211
Carbohydrate ....33 grams
Protein ....4 grams
Fat.................................7 grams (30%)

Saturated fat..................................1 gram
Cholesterol..........................0 milligrams
Fiber...4 grams
Sodium............................303 milligrams
Without added salt............15 milligrams

SWEET POTATOES WITH APPLE

8 Servings/Serving size: 1/2 cup

A camping friend brought this to brunch one day, and everyone liked it. This is sweet and tasty without added sugar.

INGREDIENTS

3	large apples, thinly sliced
1	Tbsp. lemon juice
1 1/2	lbs. sweet potatoes, peeled and sliced (long narrow ones if available; halved lengthwise if round)
1	Tbsp. reduced-calorie margarine
1/4	cup apple juice or sweet cider

METHOD

1. Coat apple slices with lemon juice.
2. Spray a casserole with nonstick vegetable cooking spray. Layer potatoes and apples in casserole. Arrange the top in a pinwheel design.
3. Dot with margarine. Pour juice over all. Cover. Bake at 350° for about 45 minutes.
4. Uncover and bake for about 15 minutes or until potatoes are done.

Starch/Bread Exchange 1	Fat..1 gram (6%)
Fruit Exchange 1	Saturated fat ....trace
Calories 157	Cholesterol...........................0 milligrams
Carbohydrate ....35 grams	Fiber...6 grams
Protein ....2 grams	Sodium............................28 milligrams

VEGETABLES DRESSED WITH ALMONDS

4 Servings/Serving size: 1/2 cup

Use vegetables in season or on special, or use whatever the garden is producing.

INGREDIENTS

1	lb. asparagus or other vegetable
2	scallions
1	tsp. peanut oil
1/4	tsp. lite soy sauce
1/8	tsp. sugar
1	Tbsp. slivered almonds

METHOD

1. Cut vegetables into slender 2-inch-long pieces. Cut diagonally for fastest cooking.
2. In wok or skillet, heat oil over high heat. Add the vegetables and cook, stirring constantly, until green vegetables turn bright green and other vegetables are tender-crisp.
3. Turn burner off. Add salt, sugar, and almonds. Stir until lightly toasted. Serve warm or cold.

⚖ Balance with lower-fat dishes on days you use this recipe.

Vegetable Exchange	1	Fat	3 grams (38%)
Fat Exchange	1/2	Saturated fat	trace
Calories	71	Cholesterol	0 milligrams
Carbohydrate	7 grams	Fiber	2 grams
Protein	4 grams	Sodium	50 milligrams

ZESTY STIR-FRIED SPINACH

6 Servings/Serving size: 1/6 recipe

All taste-testers agreed this was a winning combination. Try it when you have an abundance of spinach in your garden or it is on special where you shop.

INGREDIENTS

2	pkg. (10 oz. each) frozen or up to 2 lb. fresh spinach
2	Tbsp. peanut oil
1	clove garlic, minced
1	small onion, sliced
2	slices fresh gingerroot
8	oz. fresh mushrooms, sliced (optional)
1	Tbsp. dry sherry or white wine (optional)
1 1/2	Tbsp. lite soy sauce
1/2	tsp. sugar

METHOD

1. Wash and trim spinach. Cut or tear into strips (use kitchen shears).
2. Heat oil in large skillet with cover. Stir-fry garlic, onion, and ginger for 1 minute.
3. Add spinach and mushrooms. Stir-fry for 3 minutes.
4. Add sherry, soy sauce, and sugar. Lower heat. Cover. Cook 3 minutes.
5. Serve immediately.

⚖ Balance with lower-fat dishes on days you use this recipe.

Vegetable Exchange	1
Fat Exchange	1/2
Calories	71
Carbohydrate	7 grams
Protein	4 grams

Fat	3 grams (38%)
Saturated fat	trace
Cholesterol	0 milligrams
Fiber	4 grams
Sodium	105 milligrams

DESSERTS

DESSERTS

The dessert section is large because of the widely-held notion that to "eat light, eat right" means giving up desserts. This collection demonstrates that desserts can be an important part of a well-planned diet. Desserts can be high in fiber but low in fat, sodium, sugar, and cholesterol and still taste wonderful. The trick is to use some foods in unfamiliar ways and not to expect that every recipe will fill everyone's needs. These directions may inspire additional versions, especially as new products become available.

For example, most of the testing for breads and desserts was completed before I discovered dried egg whites. I'm sure that they could be used in many recipes with excellent results. Low-fat, low-cholesterol egg substitutes may also be used in place of whole eggs with favorable results.

APPLE CHEESECAKE PIE

8 Servings/Serving size: 1 slice

Save calories by doing without a real crust. Grape-Nuts cereal provides crunch to set off the spicy apples and creamy topping.

INGREDIENTS

2/3	cup Grape-Nuts cereal
2	large apples, peeled, cored, and thinly sliced
1	tsp. grated lemon peel
1	tsp. lemon juice
1/2	tsp. cinnamon
1 1/2	cups part-skim ricotta cheese
8	pkg. artificial sweetener
1	egg white plus
1	whole egg, lightly beaten or 1/4 cup egg substitute
1	cup low-fat plain yogurt

METHOD

1. Sprinkle the cereal on the bottom of a deep 9-inch pie pan coated with nonstick vegetable cooking spray.
2. Arrange apples over the cereal and sprinkle with the lemon peel, lemon juice, and cinnamon.
3. Combine ricotta, artificial sweetener, egg, and yogurt, mixing with a spoon until smooth. Pour over the apples.
4. Bake at 350° for 45 minutes or until apples are tender when pierced with a fork and the top is golden.
5. Serve warm or cold.

Fruit Exchange	2	Fat	5 grams (25%)
Medium-Fat Meat Exchange	1	Saturated fat	3 grams
Calories	181	Cholesterol	16 milligrams
Carbohydrate	29 grams	Fiber	3 grams
Protein	5 grams	Sodium	218 milligrams

RHUBARB-BANANA BAKE*

8 Servings/Serving size: 1/8 recipe

Banana sets off the tartness of rhubarb without the need for much added sugar. Artificial sweetener could be used in the fruit mixture with excellent results. It may be served plain or with any of the creamy dessert sauces found throughout this section.

INGREDIENTS

2 1/2 cups (about 10 oz.) diced
      rhubarb, fresh or frozen and
      thawed
2   ripe bananas, sliced
4   Tbsp. sugar, divided
1/4 tsp. cinnamon
      Generous dash nutmeg
1/2 cup whole-wheat flour
1/2 cup graham cracker crumbs
      (about 6 squares)
1 1/2 tsp. baking powder
1/4 cup reduced-calorie margarine
1/4 cup egg substitute
1/4 cup skim milk

METHOD

1. Combine the fruit, 2 Tbsp. of the sugar, cinnamon, and nutmeg. Spoon the mixture into a 9-inch pie plate or shallow baking dish coated with nonstick vegetable cooking spray.
2. Combine flour, graham cracker crumbs, and baking powder. Cut in the margarine until the mixture is crumbly.
3. Combine the egg and milk, and stir this into the flour mixture.
4. Spoon the batter as evenly as possible over the fruit mixture.
5. Sprinkle with the remaining 2 Tbsp. of sugar. Bake at 400° for 25–30 minutes.
6. Serve warm or at room temperature.

*For occasional use only, due to sugar content.

Starch/Bread Exchange 1	Fat.....................................4 grams (23%)	
Fruit Exchange 1	Saturated fat.................................1 gram	
Fat Exchange 1	Cholesterol..........................0 milligrams	
Calories 160	Fiber...3 grams	
Carbohydrate ....28 grams	Sodium...........................187 milligrams	
Protein ....3 grams		

GUILTLESS "CHEESECAKE" (COOKED)*

10 Servings/Serving size: 1 slice

Top with a few pieces of fresh fruit, such as strawberries, raspberries, blueberries, melon, oranges, kiwi, peaches, or sweet red cherries, or one of the fruit sauces in this section.

INGREDIENTS

3	whole graham crackers (6 squares)	4	strips lemon zest (the yellow part of the lemon peel)
1	Tbsp. reduced-calorie margarine	15	oz. nonfat ricotta cheese
		15	oz. part-skim ricotta cheese
3	Tbsp. sugar	1/2	cup egg substitute
4	pkg. artificial sweetener (not aspartame)	1/4	cup lemon juice

METHOD

1. Cover outside of 9-inch springform pan with foil to prevent leakage or use deep 9-inch pie pan. Break up crackers and use metal blade of food processor to process until finely chopped, about 30 seconds.
2. Add margarine and 1 Tbsp. sugar and process to combine, about 15 seconds. Press into bottom of pan and bake at 325° for 10 minutes.
3. In same bowl, process zest and the rest of the sweeteners until finely chopped, about 1 minute.
4. Add ricotta and process until very smooth, about 2 minutes, scraping bowl as necessary.
5. Add remaining ingredients and process until blended, about 15 seconds.
6. Pour into pan and bake at 325° about 45 minutes. Cool completely on wire rack, then refrigerate before serving.

*For occasional use only, due to sugar content.

Starch/Bread Exchange	1	Fat	5 grams (36%)
Medium-Fat Meat Exchange	1	Saturated fat	3 grams
Calories	125	Cholesterol	14 milligrams
Carbohydrate	12 grams	Fiber	trace
Protein	8 grams	Sodium	118 milligrams

GUILTLESS "CHEESECAKE" (UNCOOKED)*

8–10 Servings/Serving size: 1 slice

I like to make this in the summer when oven heat is unwelcome. Serve plain or with fresh fruit in season.

INGREDIENTS

1	Tbsp. reduced-calorie margarine
1/3	cup graham cracker crumbs
4	Tbsp. lemon juice
1	envelope unflavored gelatin
2	cups low-fat cottage cheese
1	cup nonfat ricotta cheese
3	Tbsp. sugar
4	pkg. artificial sweetener
1	tsp. grated lemon peel
1	tsp. vanilla

METHOD

1. Grease an 8-inch springform pan or deep 9-inch pie pan with margarine. Sprinkle the bottom and sides of pan with the graham cracker crumbs.
2. Sprinkle gelatin over lemon juice and let stand 5 minutes. Dissolve the gelatin over low heat then allow to cool but not set.
3. Puree the cottage cheese and the ricotta cheese in an electric blender or food processor until smooth.
4. Add sugar, artificial sweetener, lemon peel, and vanilla and beat until smooth.
5. Blend gelatin into cheese mixture and pour into prepared pan. Refrigerate for 3 hours or until set.

*For occasional use only, due to sugar content.

Fruit Exchange	1	Fat	1 gram (10%)
Lean Meat Exchange	1	Saturated fat	trace
Calories	89	Cholesterol	2 milligrams
Carbohydrate	9 grams	Fiber	trace
Protein	11 grams	Sodium	189 milligrams

TOFU "CHEESECAKE" WITH STRAWBERRIES*

8 Servings/Serving size: 1 slice with 2 Tbsp. glaze

Because people have asked for ways to serve tofu in disguise, I'm including this one with tofu as the main ingredient, which my most discriminating taste-tester failed to identify (he loved the results). I recommend making this early in the day and serving it that evening when there is a crowd around to eat it right up, as the crust gets soggy after sitting overnight. But it always tastes scrumptious.

INGREDIENTS

2	Tbsp. reduced-calorie margarine, divided
1	cup graham cracker crumbs
1/4	cup walnuts, finely chopped
1 1/4	lb. soft tofu, well drained
1	carton (8 oz.) low-fat lemon yogurt
1/3	cup honey
2	Tbsp. fresh lemon juice
1 1/2	tsp. vanilla
1/2	tsp. grated lemon peel

Strawberry glaze:

1	cup sliced strawberries
1/2	cup water
	Juice of half a lemon
1/8	tsp. cinnamon
1	Tbsp. cornstarch
2	Tbsp. maple syrup or other sweetener to taste

METHOD

1. In oven, melt 2 Tbsp. margarine in deep 9-inch pie plate. Add cracker crumbs and walnuts. Combine and press on bottom and up sides of pan.
2. Combine rest of ingredients in blender or food processor. Blend until smooth. Pour into pie pan. Bake at 350° for 40 minutes. Cool on rack.
3. Combine ingredients for glaze in saucepan. Cook until sauce is thick and clear. Cool to room temperature. Spread over cooled cheesecake and refrigerate. Serve when chilled.

Balance with lower-fat dishes on days you use this recipe. *For occasional use only, due to sugar content.

With glaze:

Starch/Bread Exchange	2
Medium-Fat Meat Exchange	1
Fat Exchange	1
Calories	287
Carbohydrate	35 grams
Protein	13 grams
Fat	11 grams (37%)
Saturated fat	2 grams
Cholesterol	1 gram
Fiber	1 gram
Sodium	119 milligrams

BANANA AND DATE DESSERT

5 Servings/Serving size: 1/5 recipe

INGREDIENTS

2   ripe bananas, peeled and sliced
1/2 cup dates, chopped
1   cup low-fat plain yogurt

METHOD

1. Arrange a layer of bananas in a small serving bowl.
2. Cover with dates and top with another layer of bananas.
3. Spread yogurt over fruit, cover the dish, and refrigerate for several hours to allow yogurt to absorb the flavor of the dates.

Fruit Exchange 2
Calories 129
Carbohydrate ....27 grams
Protein ....3 grams
Fat.......................................1 gram (7%)

Saturated fat.................................1 gram
Cholesterol..........................3 milligrams
Fiber..3 grams
Sodium.............................33 milligrams

FRUIT CRISP

2 Servings/Serving size: 6 oz.

Variations: Other fruits such as pears, peaches, rhubarb or berries can be substituted for apples; add raisins to fruit; add nuts to topping; serve with a dollop of low-fat plain yogurt sweetened with honey, rosewater, nutmeg, artificial sweetener, or maple syrup; or serve with one of the creamy fruit sauces in this section.

INGREDIENTS

1	large apple, sliced
2	tsp. lemon juice
2	tsp. reduced-calorie margarine
1/2	cup quick-cooking rolled oats
1 1/2	pkg. artificial sweetener (not aspartame)
1/4	tsp. cinnamon

METHOD

1. Divide apple slices equally between two 6-oz. custard cups. Sprinkle each with lemon juice.
2. Microwave margarine in a small dish 15–20 seconds on HIGH or until softened.
3. Mix in oats, brown sugar and cinnamon. Spoon evenly over apples.
4. Microwave both dishes 2–3 minutes on HIGH or until apples are tender. Serve warm.

Starch/Bread Exchange	1	Fat	2 grams (13%)
Fruit Exchange	1	Saturated fat	1 gram
Calories	138	Cholesterol	0 milligrams
Carbohydrate	27 grams	Fiber	3 grams
Protein	3 grams	Sodium	41 milligrams

APPLES 'N NECTAR

4 Servings/Serving size: 1 apple

Nice to make when you have a little extra time to cook for someone special.

INGREDIENTS

1 1/2 cups unsweetened apricot and orange nectar or unsweetened orange juice
2   Tbsp. golden raisins
1   Tbsp. reduced-calorie margarine
4   Granny Smith or other crisp dessert apples
1   Tbsp. cornstarch

METHOD

1. Bring fruit juices, raisins, and margarine to a boil.
2. Halve, peel, and core apples. Lower them carefully into juice mixture and simmer gently for 7–10 minutes or until soft but not mushy.
3. Mix cornstarch with a little cold water to make a paste.
4. Transfer apples to a serving dish, cut side down.
5. Stir the cornstarch mixture into the juice and simmer for 2–3 minutes. Pour over apples and chill before serving.

Fruit Exchange 2	Saturated fat ....trace
Calories 162	Cholesterol...........................0 milligrams
Carbohydrate ....35 grams	Fiber..4 grams
Protein....................................1 gram	Sodium..............................31 milligrams
Fat...................................2 grams (11%)	

FROZEN TOFU CHERRY CUPS

6 Servings/Serving size: 1 cup

Use these directions as a basic guide for fruits and flavorings of your choice. This mix also makes healthful popsicles that do not drip.

INGREDIENTS

12	oz. soft tofu, drained
2	Tbsp. honey
1	tsp. almond extract
2	crisp almond or pecan cookies, crushed
20	dark sweet cherries, halved and pitted
6	cherries with stems for garnish

METHOD

1. In food processor, process tofu, honey, almond flavoring, and half the cookies.
2. Fold in cherry halves.
3. Spoon into paper-lined muffin cups and sprinkle with remaining crumbs.
4. Cover and freeze 2 hours or until firm.
5. Soften at room temperature 5–8 minutes before serving. Garnish with whole cherries.

⚖ Balance with lower-fat dishes on days you use this recipe.

Medium-Fat Meat Exchange	1	Fat	7 grams (39%)
Starch/Bread Exchange	1	Saturated fat	1 gram
Calories	163	Cholesterol	0 milligrams
Carbohydrate	15 grams	Fiber	1 gram
Protein	10 grams	Sodium	22 milligrams

DELUXE CARROT CAKE

16 Servings/Serving size: 1 slice

Serve thin slices for a large gathering that has eaten a hearty main course. Serve thick slabs to fewer people who have had a rather light main course. Pass Maple/Yogurt Sauce if desired: Stir together 1/2 cup low-fat plain yogurt, 2 tsp. maple syrup, and a couple drops of vanilla and chill.

INGREDIENTS

1	can (20 oz.) crushed pineapple in unsweetened juice, divided	2	tsp. vanilla
		1	cup unsweetened coconut
		3/4	cup raisins
2	cups flour		
1	cup nonfat powdered milk		
2	tsp. baking powder	**Frosting:**	
2	tsp. cinnamon	1	cup nonfat ricotta cheese
1/2	cup walnuts, chopped	4	packets artificial sweetener
2	cups carrots, shredded	2	tsp. vanilla
3/4	cup egg substitute	1	cup crushed pineapple packed in unsweetened juice, drained
1/3	cup corn oil		

METHOD

1. Drain juice from pineapple. Reserve one half of the drained pineapple for the filling.
2. Sift together flour, powdered milk, baking powder, and cinnamon.
3. Add walnuts and carrots.
4. In a separate bowl, mix together eggs, juice, oil, and vanilla.
5. Blend the two mixtures together until just combined. Fold in 1 cup drained pineapple, coconut, and raisins.
6. Pour into two 9-inch round cake pans that have been coated with nonstick vegetable cooking spray and floured. Bake at 350° for 40 minutes. Let cool 10 minutes in pans, then remove and cool completely on racks before frosting.
7. For Frosting, beat ricotta, sweetener, and vanilla until fluffy, then stir in pineapple. Spread between layers.

⚖ Balance with lower-fat dishes on days you use this recipe.

Starch/Bread Exchange	2	Fat	10 grams (37%)
Fat Exchange	2	Saturated fat	3 grams
Calories	262	Cholesterol	2 milligrams
Carbohydrate	32 grams	Fiber	1 gram
Protein	11 grams	Sodium	142 milligrams

CARROT CAKE WITH VARIATIONS

16 Servings/Serving size: 1 slice

Enjoy this vitamin-rich cake without worrying about cholesterol and fat.

INGREDIENTS

1 1/2 cups flour	1 cup unsweetened applesauce or 1 cup crushed pineapple in unsweetened pineapple juice
1/2 cup whole-wheat flour	
1/3 cup sugar	
8 packets artificial sweetner	
2 tsp. baking soda	1/4 cup corn oil
1 1/2 tsp. cinnamon	1 tsp. vanilla
1/2 tsp. nutmeg	2 egg whites
1/4 tsp. cloves (optional)	2 eggs
1/2 tsp. salt (optional)	3 cups carrots, coarsely grated (about 3/4 pound)

METHOD

1. Sift the dry ingredients into a large mixing bowl.
2. Combine the applesauce, oil, vanilla, and eggs and add them to the flour mixture, stirring until the ingredients are well blended.
3. Add the carrots and mix again.
4. Pour the batter into a 9-inch tube pan coated with nonstick vegetable cooking spray. Bake at 350° for 1 hour or until a toothpick inserted in thickest part of cake comes out clean. Set the cake pan on a wire rack for 5 minutes. Then remove cake from pan. Or pour batter into a microwave-safe tube pan and microwave for about 10–12 minutes.

Fat Exchange 1	Saturated fat................................1 gram
Starch/Bread Exchange......................1	Cholesterol........................27 milligrams
Calories 128	Fiber ....1 gram
Carbohydrate ....20 grams	Sodium..........................198 milligrams
Protein......................................3 grams	Without added salt......... 126 milligrams
Fat................................4 grams (28%)	

BAKED APPLES

2 Servings/Serving size: 1 apple

Variations: Serve baked apples with low-fat plain yogurt flavored with brown sugar substitute and cinnamon or add raisins to center of apples.

INGREDIENTS

2   baking apples
1 1/2 packets artificial sweetener
     (not aspartame)
3   Tbsp. apple juice or orange
     juice

METHOD

1. Wash and core apples and place in baking dish.
2. Combine the artificial sweetener with the juice. Pour over apples.
3. Cover. Microwave 3–4 minutes on HIGH. Let stand 3 minutes.

Fruit Exchange 1 1/2
Calories 88
Carbohydrate ....22 grams
Protein ....0 grams
Fat ....0 grams (0%)

Saturated fat ....0 grams
Cholesterol ....0 milligrams
Fiber ....3 grams
Sodium ....1 milligram

SPRING RHUBARB CAKE WITH FROSTING*

18 Servings/Serving size: 1 slice

This luscious, moist cake deserves a tender offering from your rhubarb patch. It takes 5 medium size stalks (13 inches long x 1/2 inch in diameter). Tip: To use dry buttermilk, sift buttermilk powder with dry ingredients and use a scant 1 cup of water when mixing.

INGREDIENTS

1 1/4 cups flour
3/4 cup whole-wheat flour
1 tsp. baking powder
1/2 tsp. baking soda
1/4 tsp. cinnamon
1/8 tsp. salt (optional)
1/2 cup reduced-calorie margarine
1/2 cup packed dark brown sugar
1/4 cup white sugar or noncaloric sweetener

1 egg
1 tsp. vanilla
1 cup buttermilk
2 cups (about 10 oz.) finely diced rhubarb, fresh or frozen

Topping:
1/4 cup brown sugar
1 1/2 tsp. cinnamon
1/2 cup walnuts, chopped

METHOD

1. Sift together the flours with the baking powder, baking soda, 1/4 tsp. cinnamon, and salt.
2. In a large mixing bowl, beat the margarine with 1/2 cup brown sugar and white sugar or substitute.
3. Add the egg and vanilla and beat the mixture until it is fluffy. To this mixture alternately add the flour mixture and the buttermilk; beat the ingredients until they are well mixed.
4. Stir in the rhubarb; pour the batter into a 9 x 13-inch baking pan coated with nonstick vegetable cooking spray.
5. Mix together the topping ingredients and sprinkle evenly over the batter. Bake at 350° for 35–40 minutes or until a toothpick inserted in the center of the cake comes out clean.

*For occasional use only, due to sugar content.

Starch/Bread Exchange 1	Saturated fat.................................1 gram
Fat Exchange 1	Cholesterol........................12 milligrams
Calories 149	Fiber ....1 gram
Carbohydrate ....22 grams	Sodium...........................120 milligrams
Protein ....4 grams	Without added salt..........104 milligrams
Fat....................................5 grams (30%)	

PERSIAN FRUIT DELIGHT

4 Servings/Serving size: 1/4 recipe

A refreshing fruit dessert for a hot day. Rosewater may be found in the health food store.

INGREDIENTS

2   ripe peaches
2   cups cantaloupe or melon, in
     cubes or balls, with juice
1/2–1 tsp. rosewater

METHOD

1. Slice peaches into your prettiest glass bowl, saving all the juice.
2. Add cantaloupe.
3. Sprinkle with rosewater.
4. Refrigerate for a few hours.
5. Stir and serve in thin long-stemmed goblets.

Fruit Exchange	1	Saturated fat	0 gram
Calories	88	Cholesterol	0 milligrams
Carbohydrate	20 grams	Fiber	3 grams
Protein	2 grams	Sodium	24 milligrams
Fat	0 grams (0%)		

LINDA'S CHOCOLATE LOG

8 Servings/Serving size: 1 slice

A jelly roll pan is the same as a cookie pan with edges that stand up on all four sides. Some cookie pans have one end open so cookies can slide off the pan.

INGREDIENTS

1	banana fresh or frozen, thawed	Filling:	
2	slices bread, white or whole-wheat, cubed	1/2	cup part-skim ricotta cheese
2	pkg. (0.75 oz. each) diet chocolate milk shake mix	1	tsp. vanilla
1/2	cup egg substitute	4	packets artificial sweetener
1/2	tsp. cream of tartar		
1/2	tsp. baking soda		
1	tsp. vanilla		

METHOD

1. Combine cake ingredients in a blender or food processor and blend until smooth.
2. Spray jelly roll pan with nonstick vegetable cooking spray. Pour mixture into pan and spread to corners. Cook at 350° for 10 minutes.
3. Let stand 1–2 minutes. Remove from pan and cool. Prepare filling.
4. Blend filling ingredients. Spread on cake and roll up.
5. Wrap in foil and refrigerate or cut in slices and serve immediately. Serve on dessert plates plain or topped with sliced fruit or a fruit sauce.

Starch/Bread Exchange	1	Saturated fat	1 gram
Calories	62	Cholesterol	5 milligrams
Carbohydrate	11 grams	Fiber	1 gram
Protein	4 grams	Sodium	187 milligrams
Fat	2 grams (29%)		

GWEN'S STRAWBERRY RHUBARB SAUCE

32 Servings /Serving size: 1/4 cup

Serve in sauce dishes plain; with yogurt or cottage cheese; as a spread on toast or English muffins, pancakes, waffles; or as a topping for cheesecake.

INGREDIENTS

8   **cups sliced rhubarb, fresh or frozen**

1   **small pkg. (makes 2 cups) diet strawberry gelatin**

1   **can (8 oz.) crushed pineapple in unsweetened juice**

METHOD

1. Simmer rhubarb in 1/2–1 cup water until rhubarb is soft. Remove from heat.
2. Stir in gelatin and pineapple with juice. Refrigerate.

Free Food

Calories 16	Saturated fat ....0 grams
Carbohydrate ....4 grams	Cholesterol..........................0 milligrams
Protein ....0 grams	Fiber ....1 gram
Fat.....................................0 grams (0%)	Sodium...............................7 milligrams

4 Servings/Serving size: 1/4 recipe

Variations: Custard can also be cooked in four 6-oz. custard cups: microwave 5–8 minutes on MEDIUM (50% power) or until almost set in center, rearrange cups halfway through cooking, and remove individual custards from oven as they finish cooking. Then add a drop or two of maple flavoring or serve with one of the fruit sauces described in this section.

INGREDIENTS

1 3/4 cups low-fat milk
6   packets artifical sweetener
3/4   cup egg substitute
1/4   tsp. salt (optional)
1/4   tsp. vanilla
       Nutmeg

METHOD

1. Place milk in 1 1/2-qt. bowl. Microwave 3–3 1/2 minutes on HIGH or until hot but not boiling.
2. Add remaining ingredients except nutmeg; beat well. Sprinkle with nutmeg.
3. Microwave 11–15 minutes on MEDIUM (50% power), or until almost set in center. Let stand 5 minutes. Serve warm or cold.

Meat Exchange......1	Saturated fat......1 gram
Calories......91	Cholesterol......4 milligrams
Carbohydrate......7 grams	Fiber......0 grams
Protein......9 grams	Sodium......280 milligrams
Fat......3 grams (30%)	Without added salt......137 milligrams

LOW-CALORIE JAM

32 Servings/Serving size: 1 Tbsp.

Here is a fruit jam recipe that can be varied to use whatever fruit is available and to suit individual tastes. I will start you off with two combinations. Use it as a topping for cheesecake (spread before sauce is completely set); as jam on toast, muffins, bagels, or breakfast rolls; and with peanut butter for sandwiches. Requires refrigeration and will not keep as long as conventional jam. Use within 2 weeks.

INGREDIENTS

2   **cups blueberries and 2 tsp. grated orange peel, OR**

2   **cups fresh peaches, finely chopped, and 1/2 tsp. grated lemon peel, 1/2 tsp. grated lime peel, and a few gratings of fresh nutmeg**

1/3   **cup sugar**

1–2   **tsp. grated citrus peel**

1   **envelope unflavored gelatin**

1   **cup water**

METHOD

1. In medium saucepan, combine fruit and sugar, crushing fruit slightly (I use a potato masher). Cook slowly 5 minutes, then boil rapidly for 3 minutes, stirring constantly. Stir in grated peel.
2. Sprinkle gelatin over water; let stand 1 minute.
3. Add to fruit and stir over low heat for 5 minutes. Gelatin should completely dissolve. Cool to room temperature. Cover and refrigerate.

Free Food

Calories 12

Carbohydrate ....3 grams

Protein ....0 grams

Fat ....0 grams (0%)

Saturated fat ....0 grams

Cholesterol...........................0 milligrams

Fiber...trace

Sodium ....trace

FROZEN BANANA YOGURT*

6 Servings/Serving size: 1 popsicle

Healthful treats to keep on hand in the freezer for the popsicle crowd (of all ages). Variation: If flavored, sweetened yogurts and other fruit are used, honey or other sweeteners will not be needed.

INGREDIENTS

1   large banana, fresh or frozen
1   cup (8 oz.) low-fat plain
    yogurt
3   Tbsp. honey or other
    sweetener

METHOD

1. Slice bananas and drop in blender jar or food processor bowl. If using frozen banana, partially thaw, snip off end of skin, and squeeze directly into food container.
2. Add remaining ingredients. Blend until smooth.
3. Freeze until mushy. Beat and pour into popsicle molds.
4. Freeze until firm. To unmold, hold in hand or let set at room temperature until mold will slide off. Enjoy.

*For occasional use only, due to sugar content.

Fruit Exchange 1	Saturated fat ....trace
Calories 89	Cholesterol..........................2 milligrams
Carbohydrate ....18 grams	Fiber ....1 gram
Protein.......................................2 grams	Sodium..............................27 milligrams
Fat.....................................1 gram (11 %)	

APPLESAUCE-RAISIN SQUARES*

16 Servings/Serving size: 1 square

Moist and flavorful dessert squares that bake nicely as part of an oven meal. Energy-saving tip: If oven is to be heated for just this one dish, spread the dough in an 8 x 10-inch glass oblong dish, lower the heat to 325°, and bake the squares for 20–25 minutes.

INGREDIENTS

1/4	cup egg substitute	1/2	cup bran
1/4	cup corn oil	1	cup whole-wheat flour
1/2	cup low-fat plain yogurt	1	tsp. baking powder
2/3	cup brown sugar	2	tsp. ground cinnamon
1	cup unsweetened applesauce	1	tsp. ground ginger
1	tsp. vanilla	1/4	tsp. ground nutmeg
1	tsp. lemon peel, grated	1/4	cup almonds or walnuts,
1/2	cup raisins		sliced

METHOD

1. In large mixing bowl, beat egg, oil, yogurt, brown sugar, applesauce, vanilla, and lemon peel. Add raisins and bran; mix well.
2. Sift the flour, baking powder, and spices into wet ingredients and mix only until combined.
3. Spoon into 8-inch square cake pan coated with nonstick vegetable cooking spray. Lightly press nuts into top of batter. Bake at 350° for 45 minutes or until tester inserted in center comes out clean. Let cool, then cut into squares (squares will be moist).

*For occasional use only, due to sugar content.

Starch/Bread Exchange	1	Fat	5 grams (32%)
Fat Exchange	1	Saturated fat	1 gram
Calories	141	Cholesterol	trace
Carbohydrate	21 grams	Fiber	2 grams
Protein	3 grams	Sodium	53 milligrams

WHOLE-WHEAT APPLE COOKIES*

30 cookies/Serving size: 2 cookies

INGREDIENTS

1/2	cup whole-wheat flour
1/2	cup flour
1/2	tsp. baking soda
1/2	tsp. ground cinnamon
1/4	tsp. ground cloves
1/4	cup brown sugar
1	pkg artificial sweetener
2	Tbsp. corn oil
1	egg white
1	cup apple, finely chopped
1/3	cup walnuts, finely chopped

METHOD

1. Sift together flour, soda, and spices.
2. Stir in sugar, artificial sweetener, oil, and egg.
3. Fold in apple and nuts.
4. Drop by the rounded teaspoonful onto a cookie sheet sprayed with nonstick vegetable cooking spray. Bake at 375° for 10 minutes or until lightly browned. Or arrange 8 cookies in a circle on microwave safe pan. (You can turn a casserole upside down.) Cook on HIGH for 2 minutes. Serve warm.

⚖ Balance with lower-fat dishes on days you use this recipe. *For occasional use only, due to sugar content.

Starch/Bread Exchange	1	Fat	4 grams (39%)
Fat Exchange	1	Saturated fat	trace
Calories	92	Cholesterol	0 milligrams
Carbohydrate	12 grams	Fiber	1 gram
Protein	2 grams	Sodium	33 milligrams

CARROT-OATMEAL COOKIES*

36 cookies/Serving size: 2 cookies

Taste testers liked these for coffee break time.

INGREDIENTS

1/3 cup corn oil	1/4 tsp. nutmeg
1/4 cup brown sugar	1/4 cup nonfat powdered milk
1/4 cup molasses	1/2 tsp. salt (optional)
1 egg white or 1/4 cup egg substitute	1/4 tsp. cinnamon
	1 cup carrots (2 medium-large), grated
1 cup flour	
1/2 tsp. baking powder	1/3 cup raisins
1/2 tsp. baking soda	1 1/4 cups quick-cooking rolled oats

METHOD

1. Beat together the oil, brown sugar, molasses, and egg white or substitute.
2. Sift the flour, baking powder, baking soda, nutmeg, dry milk, salt, and cinnamon into the oil mixture. Stir to combine.
3. Add the carrots, raisins, and oats and stir to mix well. Drop dough by the rounded teaspoonful about 2 inches apart onto baking sheets coated with nonstick vegetable cooking spray.
4. Bake at 375° for 10 minutes or until lightly browned around the edges.

⚖ Balance with lower-fat dishes on days you use this recipe. *For occasional use only, due to sugar content.

Starch/Bread Exchange 1	Saturated fat..................................1 gram
Fat Exchange 1	Cholesterol ....trace
Calories 129	Fiber..trace
Carbohydrate ....18 grams	Sodium....................118 milligrams
Protein ....3 grams	Without added salt............54 milligrams
Fat...................................5 grams (35%)	

GINGERED FRUIT DIP

5 Servings/Serving Size: 1/4 cup

A dip for an appetizer tray or for a dessert that complements a variety of fresh fruit. This versatile concoction doubles as instant pudding—just put it in dessert dishes and top with fresh fruit.

INGREDIENTS

1   cup low-fat cottage cheese
1   small banana, sliced
1/8 tsp. ground ginger

METHOD

1. In blender or food processor, combine cheese, banana, and ginger.
2. Process until smooth. Chill.

Lean Meat Exchange................1	Saturated fat ....trace
Calories 57	Cholesterol..........................2 milligrams
Carbohydrate ....6 grams	Fiber...trace
Protein ....6 grams	Sodium............................148 milligrams
Fat....................................1 gram (16%)	

STRAWBERRY MILKSHAKE

1 12-oz. Serving

INGREDIENTS

1   cup skim milk
1/2 ripe banana, sliced
3–5 ripe strawberries, hulls
     removed

METHOD

1. Blend all ingredients in blender or food processor.
2. Double the recipe for 2 big shakes.

Skim-Milk Exchange 1	Fat.......................................0 grams (0%)
Fruit Exchange 1	Saturated fat ....0 grams
Calories 156	Cholesterol..........................0 milligrams
Carbohydrate ....30 grams	Fiber...3 grams
Protein ....9 grams	Sodium............................125 milligrams

DATE AND RAISIN COOKIES

36 Cookies/Serving size: 1 cookie

Filled with nutrients, these are suitable for breakfast, coffee break, and after school as well as dessert time. A friend brought these treats on a camping weekend, and all tasters approved.

INGREDIENTS

8	oz. dates
1	cup raisins
1 1/2	cups water, divided
1/3	cup corn oil
1	tsp. cinnamon
1/8	tsp. nutmeg
1	tsp. baking soda
2	egg whites
2	cups whole-wheat flour
1	tsp. baking powder

METHOD

1. Combine dates, raisins, 1 1/4 cups water, oil, and spices. Cook together for 5 minutes until mushy. Cool to room temperature.
2. Dissolve baking soda in 1/4 cup of water.
3. Add egg whites, flour, and baking powder. Mix well and add to date mixture.
4. Coat a cookie sheet with nonstick vegetable cooking spray. Drop cookie mixture by the rounded teaspoonful onto the cookie sheet.
5. Bake at 350° about 12 minutes, or until dough is set and lightly browned.

Fruit Exchange 1	Saturated fat ....trace
Calories 70	Cholesterol..........................0 milligrams
Carbohydrate ....12 grams	Fiber ....1 gram
Protein...1 gram	Sodium............................39 milligrams
Fat...................................2 grams (26%)	

COTTAGE CHEESE COOKIES

30 Cookies/Serving size: 2 cookies

These soft, cakelike cookies are packed with nutritious ingredients.

INGREDIENTS

1	cup whole-wheat flour
1/4	cup nonfat powdered milk
2	tsp. baking powder
1	tsp. cinnamon
1/4	tsp. nutmeg
1/4	tsp. salt (optional)
1/4	cup bran
1/4	cup wheat germ
1/2	cup raisins

1/4	cup reduced-calorie margarine, softened
1/2	cup low-fat cottage cheese
1/4	cup sugar
2	Tbsp. honey
1/4	cup egg substitute
1	tsp. vanilla

METHOD

1. Sift the flour, dry milk, baking powder, cinnamon, nutmeg, and salt.
2. Add bran, wheat germ, and raisins.
3. In a large mixing bowl, beat margarine and cottage cheese until smooth.
4. Add the sugar and honey and beat until fluffy.
5. Add the egg substitute and vanilla and beat the mixture again.
6. Stir the reserved flour mixture into the cottage cheese mixture until they are just blended.
7. Drop dough by the rounded teaspoonful about 2 inches apart on cookie sheets coated with nonstick vegetable cooking spray.
8. Bake at 350° for 8–10 minutes or until the edges of the cookies turn golden. Remove the cookies from the pan to a rack to cool.

Starch/Bread Exchange	1	Saturated fat	1 gram
Fat Exchange	1	Cholesterol	1 milligram
Calories	132	Fiber	2 grams
Carbohydrate	19 grams	Sodium	180 milligrams
Protein	5 grams	Without added salt	142 milligrams
Fat	4 grams (27%)		

FRUIT PLATE WITH CREAMY DESSERT SAUCE

4 Servings/Serving size: 1/4 recipe

Use any collection of fruit with various colors, shapes, and textures for this dish. Nice for brunch, as a buffet salad, or for dessert. This sauce is good on other desserts, such as Rhubarb Cake and Applesauce-Raisin Squares.

INGREDIENTS

2	ripe peaches, sliced
2	kiwi fruit, peeled and sliced
1	cup strawberries, cut in half
1	cup blueberries
1	cup low-fat cottage cheese
1/2	cup orange juice
1	Tbsp. lemon juice
1	Tbsp. light brown sugar

METHOD

1. Arrange fruit on a platter or in individual dishes.
2. Combine cheese, juice, sugar, and salt in blender. Blend at high speed until smooth and creamy.
3. Pour into a pitcher for serving at the table.

Lean Meat Exchange................................1
Fruit Exchange 2
Calories 149
Carbohydrate ....27 grams
Protein ....8 grams
Fat...................................1 gram (6%)
Saturated fat ....trace
Cholesterol ....3 grams
Fiber...5 grams
Sodium...........................192 milligrams

Sauce:
Calories 73
Carbohydrate ....9 grams
Protein ....7 grams
Fat....................................1 gram (12%)
Saturated fat ....trace
Cholesterol ....3 grams
Fiber...trace
Sodium.......................187 milligrams

YUMMY DESSERT SAUCE

24 Servings/Serving size: 1 Tbsp.

A creamy sauce that complements many desserts at only 20 calories per tablespoon. The spirits add flavor and richness without many calories.

INGREDIENTS

1	tall can (14 oz.) evaporated skim milk, undiluted
2 1/2	Tbsp. sugar
2	Tbsp. cornstarch
1/3	cup skim milk
1	tsp. vanilla
2–3	tsp. orange liqueur
1	tsp. brandy

METHOD

1. Combine the evaporated milk and sugar and place over low heat.
2. Combine the cornstarch and milk, stirring into a smooth paste.
3. Slowly add this to the heated milk and sugar, stirring constantly until the sauce thickens.
4. Add the vanilla, liqueur, and brandy.
5. Simmer the sauce 1 minute longer. Serve warm.

Free Food
Calories 20
Carbohydrate ....4 grams
Protein................................1 gram
Fat ....0 grams (0%)

Saturated fat ....trace
Cholesterol...........................0 milligrams
Fiber ....0 milligrams
Sodium ....24 milligrams

FRUIT SAUCES

6 Servings/Serving size: 2 Tbsp.

Use on desserts, pancakes, waffles, toast, and biscuits. Variation: For strawberry sauce, substitute 3/4 cup ripe strawberries for the peach.

INGREDIENTS
Peach Sauce:
1   large ripe peach
1   tsp. lime or lemon juice
     Artifical sweetener to taste
     Pinch fresh grated ginger
     (optional)
     Pinch ground cinnamon
     (optional)

METHOD
1. Wash and mash fruit. Use a blender or food processor if you have one. Sweeten to taste.

Free Food
Calories 8
Carbohydrate ....2 grams
Protein ....0 grams
Fat ....0 grams (0%)

Saturated fat ....0 milligrams
Cholesterol...........................0 milligrams
Fiber ....1 gram
Sodium ....trace

THREE-FRUIT SAUCE

8 Servings/Serving size: 1/4 cup

INGREDIENTS

1 1/4 cups apple juice, divided
1   large, tart apple, sliced
1   Tbsp. arrowroot or cornstarch
1/4   tsp. grated lemon peel
1/8   tsp. vanilla
     Dash of nutmeg
1/2   cup blueberries
1/2   cup strawberries, sliced

METHOD

1. Place 1 cup apple juice and apple in medium saucepan and bring to boil. Reduce heat, cover, and simmer for about 5 minutes or until just tender-crisp.
2. Stir arrowroot or cornstarch into the remaining 1/4 cup apple juice.
3. Add to the pan along with the lemon peel, vanilla, and nutmeg, stirring until sauce thickens.
4. Remove from heat and stir in the blueberries and strawberries.
5. Serve warm, at room temperature, or cold. Refrigerate leftover sauce.

Fruit Exchange 1
Calories 44
Carbohydrate .... 11 grams
Protein .... trace
Fat .... 0 grams (0%)

Saturated fat .... 0 grams
Cholesterol .... 0 milligrams
Fiber .... 1 gram
Sodium .... 2 milligrams

INDEX

A

APPLE
Apple-Cheese Pancakes 76
Apple Cheesecake Pie 147
Apples 'N Nectar 154
Applesauce Muffins 50
Applesauce-Oat Bread 61
Applesauce-Raisin Squares 166
Apple Oat Bread 60
Baked Apples 158
Carrot Cake 157
Carrot Salad 40
Dutch Apple Pancakes 49
Fruit Crisp 153
Gingered Fruit Dip 169
Spinach-Apple Salad 35
Sweet Potatoes with Apple 141
Three-Fruit Sauce 175
Whole-Wheat Apple Cookies 169

APPLE JUICE
Carrot Bread or Muffins 57
Whole-Wheat Fruit Bread or Muffins.....58
Zucchini Bread or Muffins 56
Three-Fruit Sauce 175

ASPARAGUS
Microwaving Vegetables 130
Mushroom-Asparagus Casserole 132
Turkey-Asparagus Brunch Bake 90
Vegetable Cream Soup 26
Vegetables Dressed w/Almonds 142

B

Baked Beans 79

BANANAS
Banana and Date Dessert 152
Frozen Banana Yogurt 165
Oat Bran Banana Muffins 53
Rhubarb Banana Bake 148
Strawberry Milkshake 169
Whole-Wheat Banana Bread.....63

BEANS
Baked Beans 79
Bean Casserole 85
Chick Pea and Spinach Soup 28
Chili w/Tofu 81
Salmon and White Bean Salad 110
Spinach, Chick Pea, & Mushroom
Salad....36
Vegetables Dressed w/Almonds 142

BEEF
Individual Meat Loaf 124
Piquant Meat Loaf 123
Sloppy Joes 125
Stuffed Acorn Squash 128
Sweet and Sour Meatballs 6
Vitamin Soup 18

BLUEBERRIES
Blueberry Salad Mold 42
Buttermilk, Bran, and Blueberry
Muffins 54
Fruit Plate 172
Low-Calorie Jam 164
Maine Blueberry Muffins 55
Three-Fruit Sauce 175
Tofu Waffles 69

BRAN
Buttermilk, Bran, and Blueberry
Muffins 54
Oat Bran Banana Muffins 53
Oven "Fried" Chicken 99
Whole-Wheat and Bran Bread 62
Whole-Wheat Bread 64

BREAD
Apple-Oat Bread 60
Applesauce-Oat Bread 61
Boston Brown Bread 71
Carrot Bread.....57
Dutch Apple Pancakes 49
Homemade Sesame Crackers 72
Granary Bread 70
MultiGrain Soda Bread 65
Naturally-Sweetened Date Bread 59
No-Knead Oatmeal Yeast Bread 67
Rolled Oats Crackers 73
Rolled Oats Yeast Bread 68
Scotch Oat Scones 66
Whole-Wheat and Fruit Bread 58
Tofu Waffles 69
Whole-Wheat Banana Bread 63
Whole-Wheat and Bran Bread 62
Whole-Wheat Bread.....64
Zucchini Bread.....56
Bread Making Tips 48

BROCCOLI
Broccoli and Mushroom Dip 9
Broccoli/Cauliflower Luncheon Soup ...25
Broccoli, Sweet Red Pepper, and
Oranges 133
Chicken and Broccoli 101
Fresh Vegetable Dippers 12
One-Pot Pork Chop Dinner 126
Oriental Stir-Fry Fish
and Vegetables 114
Stir-Fry Scallops and Broccoli 119
Turkey-Asparagus Brunch Bake 90
Vegetable Cream Soup 26

C
CABBAGE
Hot or Cold Cabbage 134
Mystery Fish Dish 118
CAKE
Carrot Cake.....157
Deluxe Carrot Cake.....156
Linda's Chocolate Log.....161
Spring Rhubarb Cake 159
CARROTS
Carrot Cake.....157
Carrot Salad 40
Carrot-Oatmeal Cookies 168
Carrots with Coriander 135
Deluxe Carrot Cake 156
Glazed Chicken.....103
Oatmeal Carrot Muffins 51
Stir-Fry Scallops and Broccoli 119
Carrot Bread or Muffins 57
CAULIFLOWER
Broccoli-Cauliflower Luncheon Soup....25
Cauliflower-Cheese Soup 27
"Creamed" Cauliflower.....84
Fresh Vegetable Dippers 12
Vegetable Cream Soup 26
CHEESE
Apple-Cheese Pancakes 76
Apple Cheesecake Pie 147
Betty's Macaroni and Cheese 86
Broccoli-Cauliflower Luncheon Soup ...25
Broccoli and Mushroom Dip 9
Cauliflower-Cheese Soup 27
Cottage Cheese Cookies 171

"Creamed" Cauliflower 84
Creamy Blue Cheese Dressing 32
Crustless Zucchini Tofu Quiche 82
Eggplant Ricotta Bake 78
French Onion Soup 24
Fruit Plate 172
Gingered Fruit Dip 169
Guiltless "Cheesecake" (Cooked) 149
Guiltless "Cheesecake" (Uncooked) 150
Halibut with a Greek Flavor 117
Hearty Zucchini Hors d'oeuvres 14
Hellenic Village Salad 38
Lentil Soup 23
Linda's Chocolate Log 161
Meatless Lasagna 87
Pasta Salad 43
Spinach and Cheese Squares 13
Spinach Onion Dip 8
Stuffed Zucchini 83
Vegetable Cream Soup 26
Yogurt Cheese "Boursin".....10
Zucchini Pizzas 11
CHICKEN BROTH
Cauliflower-Cheese Soup 27
Chicken Stock 19
Couscous Spinach Salad 41
Dieter's Delight Vegetable Soup 22
French Onion Soup 24
Lentil Soup 23
Norwegian Spinach Soup 21
Quinoa-Vegetable Salad 44
Turkish Spinach Soup 20
CHICKEN
Baked Chicken Nuggets 91
Chicken Baked in Spicy Yogurt 100
Chicken and Broccoli.....101
Chicken and Fruit Salad 97
Chicken Piquant 92
Chicken Roulades 102
Chicken Stock 19
Crispy Baked Chicken 96
Glazed Chicken.....103
Oven-"Fried" Chicken.....99
Oven-Crisp Sesame Drumsticks 98
Pita Sandwich 104

INDEX

COOKIES
    Carrot Oatmeal Cookies 168
    Cottage Cheese Cookies 171
    Date and Raisin Cookies 170
    Whole-Wheat Apple Cookies 167
CORN
    Corn Chowder 29
    Scalloped Corn.....80

D

DESSERTS (See Cakes and Cookies)
    Apple Cheesecake Pie 147
    Apples 'N Nectar.....154
    Applesauce-Raisin Squares 166
    Baked Apples 158
    Banana and Date Dessert.....152
    Blueberry Salad Mold 42
    Carrot Cake 157
    Carrot-Oatmeal Cookies 168
    Cottage Cheese Cookies 171
    Custard 163
    Date and Raisin Cookies 170
    Deluxe Carrot Cake.....156
    Frozen Banana Yogurt 165
    Frozen Tofu Cherry Cups 155
    Fruit Crisp 153
    Fruit Plate.....172
    Fruit Sauces.....174
    Gingered Fruit Dip 169
    Guiltless "Cheesecake" (Cooked).....149
    Guiltless "Cheesecake"(Uncooked).....150
    Gwen's Strawberry Rhubarb
       Sauce......162
    Linda's Chocolate Log 161
    Low-Calorie Jam 164
    Peach Sauce 174
    Persian Fruit Delight 160
    Rhubarb-Banana Bake.....148
    Spring Rhubarb Cake 159
    Strawberry Milkshake.....169
    Strawberry Sauce 174
    Three-Fruit Sauce 175
    Tofu Cheesecake w/Strawberries 151
    Whole-Wheat Apple Cookies 167
    Yummy Dessert Sauce 173

E

Eggplant Ricotta Bake.....78

F

FISH AND SEAFOOD
    Clam Dip 7
    Fish Chowder 30
    Fish Florentine 116
    Fish and Fruit Salad 115
    Fish for Two from the Microwave 111
    Fried Rice with Crabmeat.....108
    Halibut with a Greek Flavor 117
    Low Calorie Fish for Four 112
    Mystery Fish Dish 118
    Oriental Stir-Fry Fish
       and Vegetables 114
    Salmon and White Bean Salad 110
    Salmon Steak with Cucumber
       Sauce.....109
    Scallops and Braised Red Onions 113
    Scallops, Peppers, and Pasta 120
    Stir-Fry Scallops and Broccoli 119
French Onion Soup 24
Fruit — See individual fruit

G

Garden Salad 33
Garlic Potatoes 140
Gingered Fruit Dip 169
Glazed Chicken.....103
Granary Bread 70
Guiltless "Cheesecake" (Cooked) 149
Guiltless "Cheesecake" (Uncooked) 150
Gwen's Strawberry Rhubarb
    Sauce 162

H

Halibut with a Greek Flavor 117
Hellenic Village Salad 38
Homemade Sesame Crackers 72

J

Low-Calorie Jam 164

K

Kabobs, Summer Vegetable 131
Kiwi Fruit Plate 172

L

Savory Lamb Stew 127
Lentil Soup 23
Linda's Chocolate Log.....161

M

Marinated Celery 15

Mayonnaise, Eggless Tofu 37
MICROWAVE COOKING
  Baked Apples 158
  Betty's Macaroni and Cheese 86
  Crustless Zucchini Tofu Quiche 82
  Custard 163
  Fish Florentine 116
  Fish for Two.....111
  French Onion Soup 24
  Fresh Vegetable Dippers 12
  Fruit Crisp 153
  Garlic Potatoes 140
  Individual Meat Loaf 124
  Meatless Lasagna 87
  Microwaved Chicken 93, 96
  Mystery Fish Dish 118
  Piquant Meat Loaf 123
  Rolled Oats Yeast Bread 68
  Sloppy Joes 125
  Sweet and Sour Meatballs 6
  Vegetable Cream Soup 26
  Whole-Wheat Apple Cookies 167
  Zippy Potatoes 138
MUFFINS
  Applesauce Muffins 50
  Buttermilk, Bran, and Blueberry
    Muffins 54
  Carrot Muffins.....57
  Maine Blueberry Muffins 55
  Oat Bran Banana Muffins 53
  Oatmeal Carrot Muffins 51
  Whole-Wheat and Fruit Muffins.....58
  Yogurt-Oatmeal Muffins 52
  Zucchini Muffins.....56
MUSHROOMS
  Broccoli and Mushroom Dip 9
  Chicken and Broccoli.....101
  Fresh Vegetable Dippers 12
  Mushroom-Asparagus Casserole 132
  Oriental Stir-Fry Fish
    and Vegetables 114
  Summer Vegetable Kabobs 131
N
Naturally Sweetened Date Bread 59
No-Knead Oatmeal Yeast Bread 67
Norwegian Spinach Soup 21

O
OATS
  Apple-Oat Bread.....60
  Applesauce-Oat Bread 61
  Carrot-Oatmeal Cookies.....168
  Individual Meat Loaf 124
  MultiGrain Soda Bread 65
  No-Knead Oatmeal Yeast Bread 67
  Oat Bran Banana Muffins.....53
  Oatmeal Carrot Muffins 51
  Piquant Meat Loaf 123
  Rolled Oats Crackers 73
  Rolled Oats Yeast Bread 68
  Scotch Oat Scones 66
  Turkey Meatballs 94
  Yogurt-Oatmeal Muffins 52
ONIONS
  Braised Yellow Onions 136
  French Onion Soup 24
  Oven-Fried Onion Rings 137
  Scallops and Braised Red Onions 113
  Spinach Onion Dip 8
  Summer Vegetable Kabobs 131
P
PASTA AND GRAINS
  Betty's Macaroni and Cheese 86
  Couscous Spinach Salad 41
  Fried Rice with Crabmeat.....108
  Homemade Noodles 77
  Meatless Lasagna 87
  Pasta Salad 43
  Quinoa-Vegetable Salad 44
  Scallops, Peppers, and Pasta 120
  Turkey and Noodles.....105
Persian Salad 34
PORK
  Baked Beans 79
  One-Pot Pork Chop Dinner 126
POTATOES
  Garlic Potatoes 140
  Oven-Baked French Fries 139
  Sweet Potatoes w/Apple 141
  Zippy Potatoes 138
PRESSURE COOKER
  Baked Beans 79

INDEX

Q

QUICHE
  Crustless Zucchini Tofu Quiche 82
  Spinach and Cheese Squares 13
Quinoa Vegetable Salad 44

R

RHUBARB
  Fruit Crisp 153
  Gwen's Strawberry Rhubarb
    Sauce 162
  Rhubarb Banana Bake.....148
  Spring Rhubarb Cake 159
RICOTTA
  Apple-Cheese Pancakes 76
  Apple Cheesecake Pie 147
  Blueberry Salad Mold 42
  Deluxe Carrot Cake.....156
  Eggplant Ricotta Bake 78
  Guiltless "Cheesecake" (Cooked) 149
  Guiltless "Cheesecake"
    (Uncooked) 150
  Linda's Chocolate Log 161
  Turkey and Noodles 105

S

SALAD
  Blueberry Salad Mold 42
  Carrot Salad 40
  Chicken and Fruit Salad 97
  Chinese Sprout Salad 39
  Couscous Spinach Salad 41
  Garden Salad 33
  Hellenic Village Salad 38
  Pasta Salad 43
  Persian Salad 34
  Quinoa-Vegetable Salad 44
  Spinach-Apple Salad 35
  Spinach, Chick Pea, and Mushroom
    Salad 36
SALAD DRESSING
  Creamy Blue Cheese Dressing 32
  Herbed Yogurt.....104
  Lemon Dressing.....34
  Very-Low-Calorie Tomato Dressing ...45
  Yogurt Dressing for Fish 109
SALMON
  Mystery Fish Dish 118

Salmon Steak 109
Salmon and White Bean Salad 110
SAUCES
  Creamy Dessert Sauce.....172
  Cucumber/Yogurt Sauce.....109
  Curry Sauce 102
  Dipping Sauce for Chicken 91
  Gingered Fruit Dip 169
  Gwen's Strawberry Rhubarb
    Sauce.....162
  Herbed Yogurt.....104
  Low-Calorie Jam 164
  Maple Yogurt Sauce 156
  Mushroom Sauce 101
  Mustard Barbecue Sauce 93
  Peach Sauce 174
  Piquant Sauce (w/Meat Loaf) 123
  Strawberry Glaze (w/Tofu Cheese-
    cake) 151
  Strawberry Sauce 174
  Three-Fruit Sauce 175
  Vegetable Dipping Sauce.....12
  Yummy Dessert Sauce 173
SCALLOPS
  Scallops and Braised Red Onions
   113
  Scallops, Peppers, and Pasta 120
  Stir-Fry Scallops and Broccoli 119
SOUPS.....18–30
SPINACH
  Chick Pea and Spinach Soup 28
  Couscous Spinach Salad 41
  Fish Florentine 116
  Norwegian Spinach Soup 21
  Spinach-Apple Salad 35
  Spinach and Cheese Squares 13
  Spinach, Chick Pea, and Mushroom
    Salad 36
  Spinach-Onion Dip 8
  Turkish Spinach Soup 20
  Zesty Stir-Fried Spinach 143
STRAWBERRIES
  Fruit Plate.....172
  Gwen's Strawberry Rhubarb
    Sauce 162
  Three-Fruit Sauce 175

Tofu Cheesecake....151
Strawberry Jam 164
Strawberry Milkshake 169
Strawberry Sauce.....174

SUGARLESS BREADS AND DESSERTS
Apples 'n Nectar 154
Baked Apples 158
Banana and Date Dessert 152
Carrot Bread or Muffins 57
Custard 163
Date and Raisin Cookies 170
Deluxe Carrot Cake 156
Frozen Banana Yogurt 165
Gingered Fruit Dip 169
Gwen's Strawberry Rhubarb
    Sauce 162
Homemade Sesame Crackers 72
Linda's Chocolate Log 161
Naturally Sweetened Date Bread 59
Peach Sauce 174
Persian Fruit Delight 160
Strawberry Milkshake 169
Strawberry Sauce 174
Three-Fruit Sauce 175
Tofu Waffles 69
Whole-Wheat Banana Bread 63
Whole-Wheat and Fruit Bread
    or Muffins 58
Zucchini Bread or Muffins 56

T
TURKEY
Stuffed Acorn Squash.....128
Turkey-Asparagus Brunch Bake 90
Turkey Chop Suey 95
Turkey Meatballs 94
Turkey and Noodles 105
Turkey Sausage Scramble 106
TOFU
Chili with Tofu.....81
Crustless Zucchini Tofu Quiche 82
Eggless Tofu Mayonnaise 37
Frozen Tofu Cherry Cups 155
Tofu Cheesecake.....151
Tofu Waffles 69

V
Veal Scallopini 122

VEGETABLES (See also individual
    listings)
Braised Yellow Onions 136
Broccoli-Cauliflower Luncheon Soup..25
Broccoli, Sweet Red Pepper, and
    Oranges 133
Carrots with Coriander.....135
Dieter's Delight Vegetable Soup 22
French Onion Soup 24
Fresh Vegetable Dippers 12
Garlic Potatoes 140
Guidelines for Microwaving
    Vegetables 132
Hearty Zucchini Hors d'oeuvres 14
Hot or Cold Cabbage 134
Marinated Celery 15
Mushroom-Asparagus Casserole
   132
Oven-Baked French Fries 139
Oven-Fried Onion Rings 137
Scalloped Corn.....80
Summer Vegetable Kabobs 131
Sweet Potatoes w/Apple 141
Vegetable Cream Soup 26
Vegetables Dressed w/Almonds 142
Vitamin Soup 18

Z
Zesty Stir-Fried Spinach 143
Zippy Potatoes 138
Zucchini Pizzas 11
ZUCCHINI
Crustless Zucchini Tofu Quiche 82
Hearty Zucchini Hors d'oeuvres 14
Zucchini Bread or Muffins 56
Stuffed Zucchini 83
Summer Vegetable Kabobs 131
Vegetable Cream Soup 26
Zucchini Pizzas 11

Now that We've Tickled Your Taste Buds, Dig into Our Recipe-Packed Pantry of Cookbooks and Menu Planners

An eleven-volume buffet of recipes and meal plans to help keep you slim and healthy.

Our Month of Meals menu planners have revolutionized daily meal planning. Forget figuring fats, calories, and exchanges. It's all done for you–automatically.

Here's how:

1. Each menu planner offers 28 day's worth of fresh, tasty new breakfast, lunch, and dinner selections.

2. The pages are split into thirds and interchangeable (see photo), so you can flip to any combination of breakfast, lunch, and dinner.

3. No matter which combinations you choose, your nutrients and exchanges will still be correct for the entire day—automatically.

4. You can even mix and match between menu planners to create literally thousands of fresh combinations. Yes, thousands!

Month of Meals

Choose from Chicken Cacciatore, Oven Fried Fish, Sloppy Joes and more (luscious snacks, too!) Many of the more complicated menus even include recipes. A "Special Occasion" sections offers tips for brunch, parties, and restaurants to help beef up your dining options. 57 pages. Spiral-bound.
#CMPMOM
ADA Member: 9.95
Nonmember: $12.50

Month of Meals 2

A healthy diet doesn't have to keep you from your favorite restaurants. Month of Meals 2 features tips and meal suggestions for Mexican, Italian, and Chinese restaurants. you can also add Veal Piccata, Beef Burritos, Chop Suey and more to your daily meal plan. Quick-to-fix and ethnic recipes are included. 64 pages. Spiral-bound
#CMPMOM2
ADA Member: $9.95
Nonmember: $12.50

Month of Meals 3

Enjoy fast food without guilt–Month of Meals 3 shows you how. Choose from McDonald's, Wendy's, Taco Bell, and others. Also, special sections offer valuable tips: how to read ingredient labels on packages; how to prepare meals for picnics & barbecues; more. Spiral-bound. #CMPMOM3
ADA Member: $9.95
Nonmember: $12.50

Month of Meals 4

Revolutionary meal planning continues! Our "meat and potatoes" menu planner serves up a fresh month's worth of choices, including old-time favorites like Pot Roast and Meatloaf. Recipes for one or two people are featured. Hints for turning family-size meals into delicious "planned overs" (healthy left-overs) will keep those generous portions from going to waste. Spiral-bound. #CMPMOM4.
ADA Member: $9.95
Nonmember: $12.50

Month of Meals 5

Effortless meal planning for the vegetarian in you. Choose from a garden of fresh selections like Eggplant Italian, Stuffed Zucchini, Cucumbers with Dill Dressing,

many others. A special section shows you the most nutritious ways to cook with whole grains, and how to add flavor to your meals with peanuts, walnuts, pecans, pumpkin seeds, and more. Spiral-bound. #CMPMOM5
ADA Member: $9.95
Nonmember: $12.50

Choose From More Than 1,000 Flavorful Recipes in a Family of Cookbooks

Specially-developed, kitchen-tested recipes only, and each volume has a completely different set of delicious meal suggestions. Each volume has a breakdown of nutrients per serving for each recipe, plus exchange values based on the Exchange Lists for Meal Planning

Family Cookbook, Volume I

More than 250 recipes—from Chinese Ginger Chicken to Strawberry Shortcake—each economical and delicious. An encyclopedia of nutrition information, tips on eating out, brown-bagging, weight control, and exercise are featured. 388 pages. Hardcover. #CCBF1
ADA Member: $20.70
Nonmember: $23.00

Family Cookbook, Volume II

Features tips for cutting sugar, calories, and costs—plus more than 250 unforgettable recipes: Texas-Style Barbecue Sauce, Veal Cutlets, and more. An entire section is devoted to living with diabetes and gives advice on the emotional aspects of dieting. 452 pages. Hardcover. #CCBF2
ADA Member: $20.70
Nonmember: $23.00

Family Cookbook, Volume III

Add more than 200 recipes to your treasury: Broiled Scallops, Lobster Tails, and many others. Includes tips on microwaving, food processing, and freezing for fix-ahead meals. Recipes from various ethnic cuisines are also featured. 434 pages. Hardcover. #CCBF3
ADA Member: $20.70
Nonmember: $23.00

Family Cookbook, Volume IV

Recipes from Boston Scrod to Santa Fe Chicken (more than 200 in all) fill each page with great American flavor. A colorful introductory section features tidbits about the history of American cuisine. 403 pages. Hardcover. #CCBF4
ADA Member: $20.70
Nonmember: $23.00

Family Cookbook Set (YOU SAVE 10%)

Includes all four Family Cookbooks #CCBSET4
ADA Member: $74.50
Nonmember: $82.80

Holiday Cookbook

From Eggnog to Cranberry Rolls, our Holiday Cookbook will fill your table with tempting recipes from traditional Thanksgiving, Christmas, and Hanukkah feasts to savory meals for any occasion. 219 pages. Hardcover. #CCBH
ADA Member: $17.95
Nonmember: $19.95

Special Celebrations and Parties Cookbook

Whether it's a Fourth of July barbecue, Mother's Day Brunch, or birthday bash